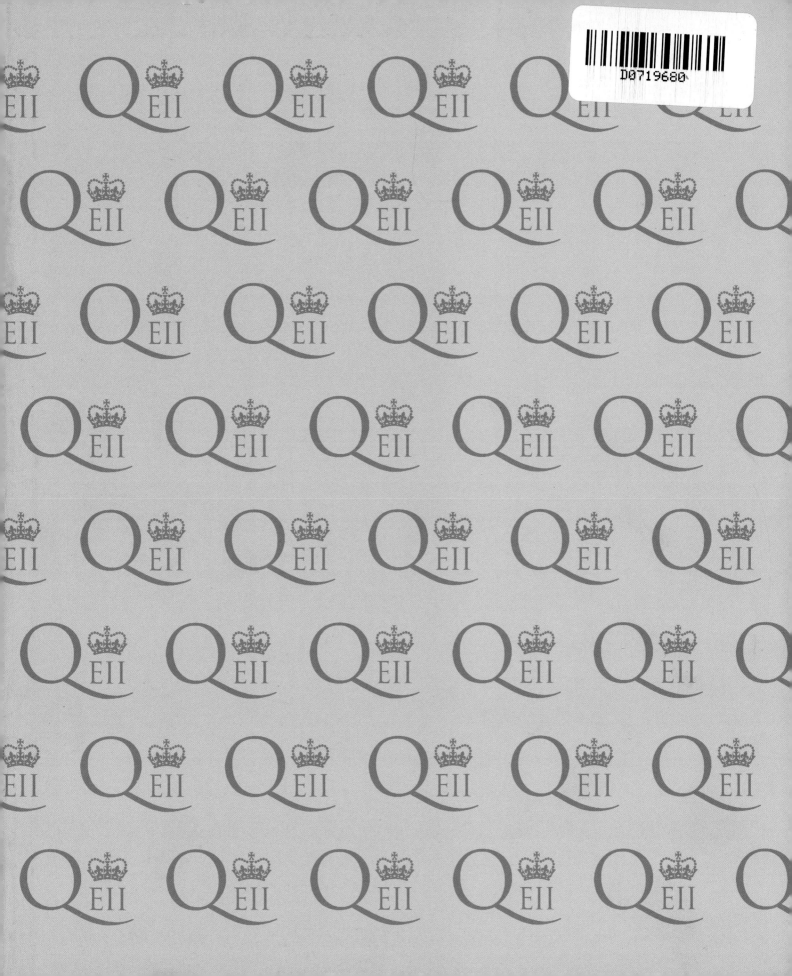

DEBRETT'S
THE QUEEN
THE DIAMOND JUBILEE

FOREWORD BY THE RT HON SIR JOHN MAJOR, KG, CH

First published in Great Britain in 2012
by Simon & Schuster UK Ltd
A CBS COMPANY

Copyright © Debrett's Limited, 2012

1 3 5 7 9 10 8 6 4 2

SIMON & SCHUSTER ILLUSTRATED BOOKS
Simon & Schuster UK Ltd
222 Gray's Inn Road
London
WC1X 8HB

www.simonandschuster.co.uk

Simon & Schuster Australia, Sydney
Simon & Schuster India, New Delhi

A CIP catalogue copy for this book is available
from the British Library

ISBN: 978-1-84983-755-2

Printed and bound by Butler Tanner and Dennis Ltd, Frome and London

DEBRETT'S

MANAGING EDITOR
Elizabeth Wyse

DESIGNER
Karen Wilks

TEXT
Rhonda Carrier
James Harpur
Charles Kidd
Elizabeth Wyse

PICTURE RESEARCH
Zooid Pictures Limited

INDEX
Christine Shaw

CHAIRMAN Conrad Free
COMMERCIAL DIRECTOR David Miller

www.debretts.com

DEBRETT'S

THE QUEEN

THE DIAMOND JUBILEE

CONTENTS

FOREWORD

by The Rt Hon Sir John Major, KG, CH

In the early hours of 21 April, 1926, in a street just off Berkeley Square, London, TRH the Duke and Duchess of York announced the birth of their first child. A daughter. Her name was Elizabeth.

No-one – least of all her parents – could have imagined the little girl, born third in line to the throne, would, one day, not only become Queen, but also one of the most widely admired, respected and longest-serving monarchs of all time.

Throughout her adult life, a remarkable sixty years of which have been on the throne, the Queen has dedicated herself to public service. You have to be approaching 70 to be able to recall any other face on British banknotes and postage stamps. Today, the world has a population of some 7 billion, the majority of whom have known no-one but the Queen as British monarch throughout their lives. She is the most widely travelled head of state in history: indeed – around the world – whenever anyone refers to "The Queen", they mean "Our Queen". Her Diamond Jubilee is, quite simply, an awe-inspiring achievement, and this magnificent book charts the course of a truly remarkable life, in pictures and print.

When the Queen took the Coronation Oath, the United Kingdom was still emerging from the aftermath of the Second World War. Her people had not forgotten the sacrifices of war. Some were still grieving for those who had perished, yet – with characteristic British spirit – were determined to pull together to lift the nation out of its economic and social gloom. The coronation inspired the British to put the grim days behind them. They looked to their monarch for example and, sixty years on, continue to do so.

Overall, throughout that period, we in the United Kingdom have been lucky. We have known peace above war; prosperity above austerity; and – whatever hardships some of us may still face – we enjoy a quality of life in 2012 that is immeasurably better than it was in 1952.

The Queen's first Prime Minister was Winston Churchill: it would be another thirteen years before her present one was born. As one of the twelve who have occupied that Office during her reign, I can say in all truth that – on matters of State – there is no-one whose counsel I would wish to seek, or whose personal judgement I would trust, more than the Queen's. It is that unique, informed, experienced, yet impartial insight which is so valuable to the Government of the United Kingdom, and yet – although a crucial aspect of her duties as monarch – it is one which remains largely unknown.

During the past 60 years we have seen many changes in every part of the world: some have been surprising, bewildering, even frightening. But amidst all the change, there has been one constant: our Queen, Elizabeth. There has been another constant, crucially important yet often unsung: HRH The Duke of Edinburgh, who has been an unfaltering and indefatigable support to the Queen. Throughout her reign, he has been the ballast of our Ship of State.

On her 21st birthday, the then Princess Elizabeth broadcast a message to the Commonwealth. She pledged: *"I declare before you all that my whole life, whether it be long or short, shall be devoted to your service ....."*

In that, HM Queen Elizabeth II has never once failed us.

THE RT HON SIR JOHN MAJOR, KG, CH
NOVEMBER 2011

A Historic Reign

With a line of descent that can be traced back to William the Conqueror, Queen Elizabeth II is the embodiment of centuries of English history. Her ancestors fought foreign wars, colonised new territories, witnessed revolutions and founded dynasties. She is preceded by two great Queens: her namesake Elizabeth I, who united a troubled kingdom and presided over a cultural renaissance, and Queen Victoria, whose longevity and dedication to family values defined an era. This rich history is symbolically interwoven into the heraldic trappings of monarchy — the royal coat of arms is an instantly recognisable assertion of the Queen's historic right to rule.

THE MONARCHS OF ENGLAND
from William the Conqueror to Richard III

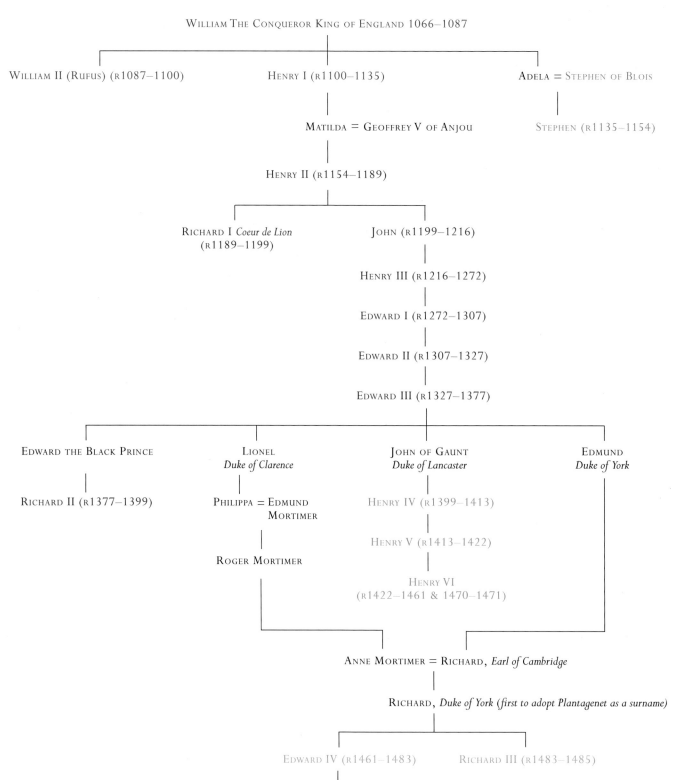

WILLIAM THE CONQUEROR KING OF ENGLAND 1066–1087

WILLIAM II (RUFUS) (R1087–1100) HENRY I (R1100–1135) ADELA = STEPHEN OF BLOIS

MATILDA = GEOFFREY V OF ANJOU STEPHEN (R1135–1154)

HENRY II (R1154–1189)

RICHARD I *Coeur de Lion* (R1189–1199) JOHN (R1199–1216)

HENRY III (R1216–1272)

EDWARD I (R1272–1307)

EDWARD II (R1307–1327)

EDWARD III (R1327–1377)

EDWARD THE BLACK PRINCE LIONEL *Duke of Clarence* JOHN OF GAUNT *Duke of Lancaster* EDMUND *Duke of York*

RICHARD II (R1377–1399) PHILIPPA = EDMUND MORTIMER HENRY IV (R1399–1413)

ROGER MORTIMER HENRY V (R1413–1422)

HENRY VI (R1422–1461 & 1470–1471)

ANNE MORTIMER = RICHARD, *Earl of Cambridge*

RICHARD, *Duke of York (first to adopt Plantagenet as a surname)*

EDWARD IV (R1461–1483) RICHARD III (R1483–1485)

HOUSE OF NORMANDY

HOUSE OF BLOIS

HOUSE OF ANJOU
LATER KNOWN AS PLANTAGENET

HOUSE OF LANCASTER

HOUSE OF YORK

This Line of Succession shows the descent of the Crown from William the Conqueror to the present sovereign, Queen Elizabeth II. It represents nearly a thousand years of monarchy, often turbulent and bloody, with ten changes of dynasty, but with only one period of non-royal rule, following the execution of King Charles I in 1649 and the establishment of the Commonwealth. This ended in 1660 when the monarchy was restored in the person of King Charles II.

William I (1028–87) the Conqueror, Duke of Normandy, took the throne by conquest, defeating Harold Godwinson, King of the English, at the Battle of Hastings in 1066. He was crowned in Westminster Abbey on Christmas Day in the same year. In 1086 he ordered the compilation of the Domesday Book, which recorded details of land settlement throughout his new realm.

King Richard I (1157–1199) known to history as Richard Coeur de Lion. Son of Henry II and his queen Eleanor of Aquitaine, Richard was induced by his mother to join his brothers in rebellion against their father. In all his life he never spent a full year in England, but his crusade against Saladin in 1191 won him the admiration of the kingdom.

Edward III (1312–77), son of Edward II and his queen Isabella of France. He claimed the throne of France in right of his mother, and, with his son Edward the Black Prince (shown here being granted the principality of Aquitaine), inflicted significant defeats on the French at Crécy, Calais and Poitiers. His kingdom suffered the Black Death 1348–50, which carried off a third of the population.

King Henry V (1387–1422). A skilled soldier, his unlikely victory over the French at Agincourt in 1415, which he won against the odds, is one of the most notable in English military history. In 1420 he was recognised as regent and 'heir of France', and married the French king's daughter, Catherine of Valois, but he never wore the French crown.

MONARCHS
from Henry VII to Queen Victoria

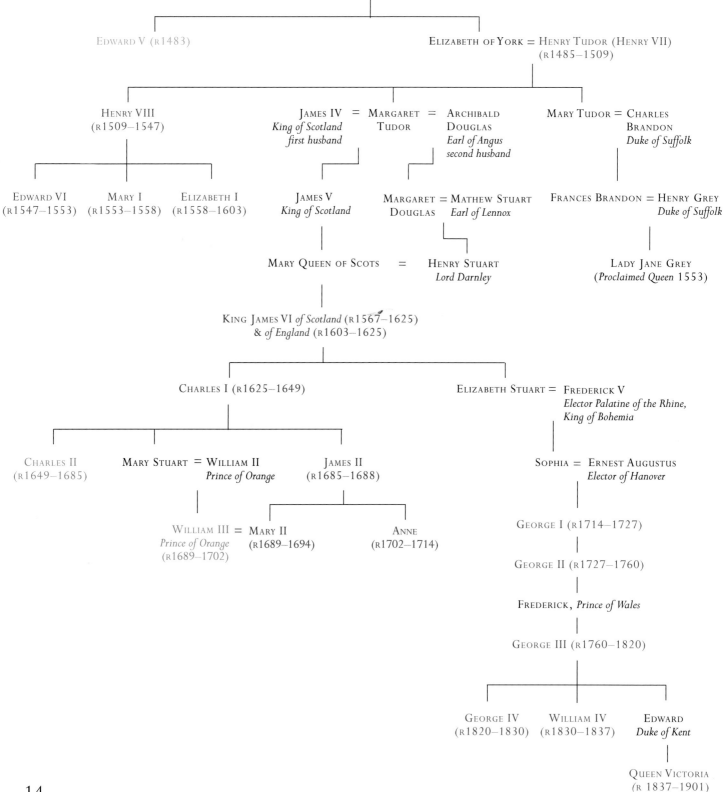

EDWARD V (R1483)

ELIZABETH OF YORK = HENRY TUDOR (HENRY VII) (R1485–1509)

HENRY VIII (R1509–1547)

JAMES IV *King of Scotland first husband* = MARGARET TUDOR = ARCHIBALD DOUGLAS *Earl of Angus second husband*

MARY TUDOR = CHARLES BRANDON *Duke of Suffolk*

EDWARD VI (R1547–1553)

MARY I (R1553–1558)

ELIZABETH I (R1558–1603)

JAMES V *King of Scotland*

MARGARET DOUGLAS = MATHEW STUART *Earl of Lennox*

FRANCES BRANDON = HENRY GREY *Duke of Suffolk*

MARY QUEEN OF SCOTS = HENRY STUART *Lord Darnley*

LADY JANE GREY *(Proclaimed Queen 1553)*

KING JAMES VI *of Scotland* (R1567–1625) & *of England* (R1603–1625)

CHARLES I (R1625–1649)

ELIZABETH STUART = FREDERICK V *Elector Palatine of the Rhine, King of Bohemia*

CHARLES II (R1649–1685)

MARY STUART = WILLIAM II *Prince of Orange*

JAMES II (R1685–1688)

SOPHIA = ERNEST AUGUSTUS *Elector of Hanover*

WILLIAM III *Prince of Orange* (R1689–1702) = MARY II (R1689–1694)

ANNE (R1702–1714)

GEORGE I (R1714–1727)

GEORGE II (R1727–1760)

FREDERICK, *Prince of Wales*

GEORGE III (R1760–1820)

GEORGE IV (R1820–1830)

WILLIAM IV (R1830–1837)

EDWARD *Duke of Kent*

QUEEN VICTORIA (R 1837–1901)

HOUSE OF YORK

HOUSE OF TUDOR

HOUSE OF STUART

HOUSE OF ORANGE

HOUSE OF HANOVER

Until the reign of Mary I the idea of a female monarch was generally considered to be unacceptable. Matilda, daughter and heiress of King Henry I, never received the wholehearted backing of the nobles and was forced to cede the Crown to her cousin Stephen of Blois. Her son, however, succeeded as Henry II and founded the royal House of Anjou. Other female heirs whose marriages brought dynastic changes in the Line of Succession include Elizabeth of York (Tudor), Mary Queen of Scots (Stuart), Sophia of Bohemia (Hanover) and Victoria (Saxe-Coburg and Gotha).

Henry VIII (1491–1547) came to the throne in 1509 on a wave of popular enthusiasm, after the parsimonious reign of his usurper father, Henry VII. Handsome and accomplished, he created the most brilliant court in Europe, but his reign is chiefly remembered for his six marriages and the separation of the Church of England from the Roman Catholic Church.

Charles I (1600–1649), was one of the most tragic figures in English history. He allowed himself to be influenced by his Catholic wife, Henrietta Maria of France, and his insistence on the divine right of kings led to civil war between the Royalists and the Parliamentarians, ending in his execution at Whitehall in 1649 and an eleven-year interregnum.

William III of Orange (1650–1702) and his wife Mary II succeeded to the throne in 1689 after her father King James II was declared by Act of Parliament to have abdicated. King James's attempt to regain the throne ended in defeat at the Battle of the Boyne 1690. William and Mary were first cousins, both Protestant, and the only joint British monarchs.

George III (1738–1820) presided over victory in the Napoleonic Wars, the Industrial Revolution, a growing empire, and the loss of the American colonies. In private he jocularly referred to his wife, Queen Charlotte, as 'Mrs King'. They had nine sons and six daughters. His latter years were marred by bouts of 'madness' probably caused by porphyria.

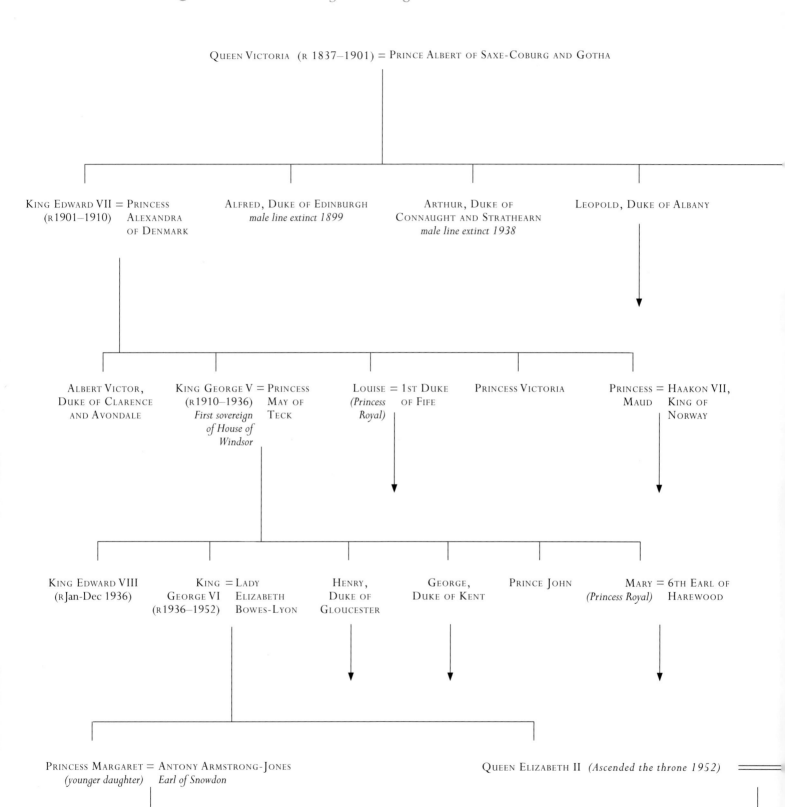

QUEEN VICTORIA AND HER DESCENDANTS

The Queen and the Duke of Edinburgh are third cousins

QUEEN VICTORIA (R 1837–1901) = PRINCE ALBERT OF SAXE-COBURG AND GOTHA

KING EDWARD VII = PRINCESS
(R1901–1910) ALEXANDRA
OF DENMARK

ALFRED, DUKE OF EDINBURGH
male line extinct 1899

ARTHUR, DUKE OF
CONNAUGHT AND STRATHEARN
male line extinct 1938

LEOPOLD, DUKE OF ALBANY

ALBERT VICTOR,
DUKE OF CLARENCE
AND AVONDALE

KING GEORGE V = PRINCESS
(R1910–1936) MAY OF
First sovereign TECK
of House of
Windsor

LOUISE = 1ST DUKE
(Princess OF FIFE
Royal)

PRINCESS VICTORIA

PRINCESS = HAAKON VII,
MAUD KING OF
NORWAY

KING EDWARD VIII
(RJan-Dec 1936)

KING = LADY
GEORGE VI ELIZABETH
(R1936–1952) BOWES-LYON

HENRY,
DUKE OF
GLOUCESTER

GEORGE,
DUKE OF KENT

PRINCE JOHN

MARY = 6TH EARL OF
(Princess Royal) HAREWOOD

PRINCESS MARGARET = ANTONY ARMSTRONG-JONES
(younger daughter) *Earl of Snowdon*

QUEEN ELIZABETH II *(Ascended the throne 1952)*

QUEEN VICTORIA
(1819–1901)

Queen Victoria is the longest reigning monarch in British history. Her reign saw Britain become the richest country in the world, thanks to improved industry, and her proclamation as Empress of India in 1877 marked the apogee of the British Empire. Queen Victoria's devotion to her husband, Prince Albert (created Prince Consort in 1857), and her despair at his premature death in 1861, led to her partial retreat from public life for the remaining 40 years of her reign.

VICTORIA = FREDERICK
(*Princess* III,
Royal) EMPEROR
OF
GERMANY,
KING OF
PRUSSIA

PRINCESS = LOUIS IV,
ALICE GRAND
DUKE OF
HESSE

PRINCESS = PRINCE
HELENA CHRISTIAN
OF
SCHLESWIG
-HOLSTEIN

PRINCESS LOUISE
(DUCHESS OF ARGYLL)

PRINCESS = PRINCE
BEATRICE HENRY OF
BATTENBURG

PRINCESS VICTORIA = ADMIRAL OF THE FLEET   OTHERS
OF HESSE   PRINCE LOUIS OF
BATTENBURG

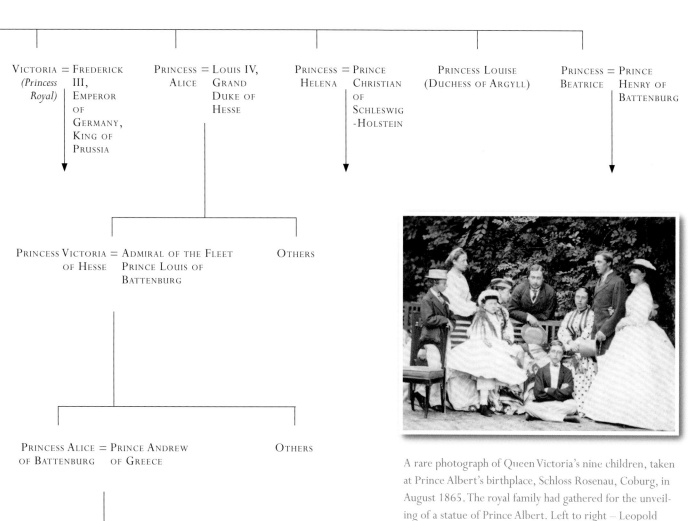

PRINCESS ALICE = PRINCE ANDREW   OTHERS
OF BATTENBURG   OF GREECE

A rare photograph of Queen Victoria's nine children, taken at Prince Albert's birthplace, Schloss Rosenau, Coburg, in August 1865. The royal family had gathered for the unveiling of a statue of Prince Albert. Left to right – Leopold (who had fallen on the Royal Yacht on the way to Germany and injured his knee. He was unable to stand – hence the chair), Louise, Beatrice, Alice, Bertie (later Edward VII), Arthur (seated on the ground), Vicky, Alfred and Helena.

PRINCE PHILIP, DUKE OF EDINBURGH

THE QUEEN'S AND PRINCESS MARGARET'S DESCENDANTS

A royal dynasty

This pedigree shows the descendants of King George VI, and the first 19 in line to the throne. The Queen is the senior representative of Queen Victoria, but other descendants, who are more distantly in the Line of Succession, include Harald V, King of Norway, Michael, King of Romania, Alexander, Crown Prince of Yugoslavia, Carl XVI Gustaf, King of Sweden, Margrethe II, Queen of Denmark, Ernst August, Prince of Hanover, Constantine II, King of the Hellenes, and Juan Carlos I, King of Spain.

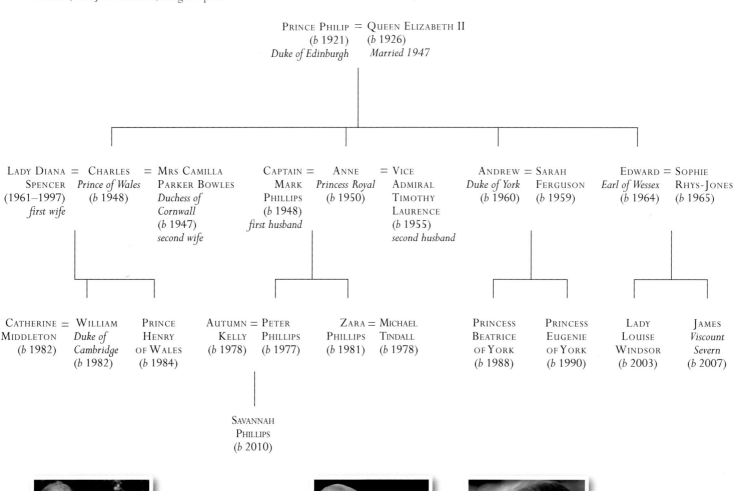

PRINCE PHILIP = QUEEN ELIZABETH II
(*b* 1921)   (*b* 1926)
Duke of Edinburgh   *Married 1947*

LADY DIANA = CHARLES = MRS CAMILLA
SPENCER   *Prince of Wales*   PARKER BOWLES
(1961–1997)   (*b* 1948)   *Duchess of Cornwall*
first wife   (*b* 1947)
second wife

CAPTAIN = ANNE = VICE
MARK   *Princess Royal*   ADMIRAL
PHILLIPS   (*b* 1950)   TIMOTHY
(*b* 1948)   LAURENCE
first husband   (*b* 1955)
second husband

ANDREW = SARAH
Duke of York   FERGUSON
(*b* 1960)   (*b* 1959)

EDWARD = SOPHIE
Earl of Wessex   RHYS-JONES
(*b* 1964)   (*b* 1965)

CATHERINE = WILLIAM
MIDDLETON   *Duke of Cambridge*
(*b* 1982)   (*b* 1982)

PRINCE
HENRY
OF WALES
(*b* 1984)

AUTUMN = PETER
KELLY   PHILLIPS
(*b* 1978)   (*b* 1977)

ZARA = MICHAEL
PHILLIPS   TINDALL
(*b* 1981)   (*b* 1978)

PRINCESS
BEATRICE
OF YORK
(*b* 1988)

PRINCESS
EUGENIE
OF YORK
(*b* 1990)

LADY
LOUISE
WINDSOR
(*b* 2003)

JAMES
Viscount Severn
(*b* 2007)

SAVANNAH
PHILLIPS
(*b* 2010)

Princess Elizabeth and Princess Margaret

The succession to the British throne is governed by common law and by statute. The succession follows male-preference primogeniture, in other words a male heir takes precedence over his older female sibling. Unlike the former French monarchy, however, Britain's laws of succession never included the Salic law, whereby a female heir was excluded from acceding to the throne, and which disallowed any claim to the throne through a female heir. Some of our greatest monarchs have been female: Queen Elizabeth I, Queen Victoria and Queen Elizabeth II. It is proposed that, in the future, the laws of succession will be amended to treat male and female heirs as equal, with primogeniture the exclusive right to succession, as adopted by the constitutional monarchies in Belgium, Denmark, The Netherlands, Norway and Sweden.

THE PRINCE OF WALES

THE DUKE OF CAMBRIDGE

PRINCE HENRY OF WALES

THE DUKE OF YORK

PRINCESS BEATRICE OF YORK

PRINCESS EUGENIE OF YORK

THE EARL OF WESSEX

VISCOUNT SEVERN

LADY LOUISE WINDSOR

THE PRINCESS ROYAL

PETER PHILLIPS

SAVANNAH PHILLIPS

ZARA TINDALL

VISCOUNT LINLEY

THE HON CHARLES ARMSTRONG-JONES

THE HON MARGARITA ARMSTRONG-JONES

LADY SARAH CHATTO

SAMUEL CHATTO

ARTHUR CHATTO

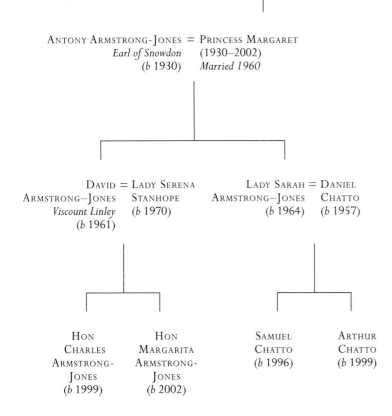

ANTONY ARMSTRONG-JONES = PRINCESS MARGARET
Earl of Snowdon   (1930–2002)
(b 1930)   *Married 1960*

DAVID = LADY SERENA   LADY SARAH = DANIEL
ARMSTRONG–JONES   STANHOPE   ARMSTRONG–JONES   CHATTO
Viscount Linley   *(b 1970)*   *(b 1964)*   *(b 1957)*
(b 1961)

HON   HON   SAMUEL   ARTHUR
CHARLES   MARGARITA   CHATTO   CHATTO
ARMSTRONG-   ARMSTRONG-   *(b 1996)*   *(b 1999)*
JONES   JONES
(b 1999)   *(b 2002)*

GLORIANA
An illustrious predecessor

"I am come amongst you…to live or die amongst you all, to lay down my life for my God and for my kingdom and for my people, my honour, and my blood, even in the dust. I know I have the body of a weak and feeble woman, but I have the heart and stomach of a king, and of a king of England too."
Queen Elizabeth I

Below: A mid-17th-century portrait of Elizabeth I, with sceptre and orb. Up to her death in 1603, Queen Elizabeth was celebrated as a wise ruler, loved by her people, loyal to her friends, accomplished in the arts and many foreign languages. Her kingdom achieved recognition across Europe as a leading power.

Right: The 'Coronation Portrait' shows the Queen, wearing an elaborate gold gown and an ermine fur stole. She is holding the orb and sceptre, symbols of her authority. With her long, flowing hair, she is depicted as the beautiful, young 'virgin' queen; modest, but powerful, with a majestic demeanour and steely gaze.

THE ACCESSION of Queen Elizabeth II was frequently referred to by the press as heralding "a new Elizabethan Age" and, viewed from the perspective of their immediate predecessors, there are indeed some factors that unite the two sovereigns at the time of their respective accessions. The present Queen came to the throne in 1952, aged 26, only seven years after the end of a war of unremitting brutality, and after a time when the monarchy had been put under enormous stress caused by the abdication of her uncle, King Edward VIII.

Queen Elizabeth I inherited the throne from her half-sister, Queen Mary I, whose reign was irrevocably marred by the rebellion of the Kentish men in 1554, the subsequent execution of Lady Jane Grey, and finally by her persecution of her Protestant subjects (300 of whom were burned at the stake). Elizabeth I was 25 when she ascended the throne. She was a slim, flame-haired young woman in the prime of life, with a flare for pageantry and heroic gestures. She had a passionate love of her country and her countrymen, and she knew how to woo them. Queen Elizabeth II similarly impressed her public with her youth, beauty and patriotism. She had a young and dashing husband, two young children, and everything to hope for.

ELISABET. D. G. ANG. FRAN. ET. HIB.
REGINA. FIDEI CHRISTIANÆ. PROPVGNA:
TRIX ACERRIMA.

THE ROYAL ARMS
Heraldic symbols

ELIZABETH II, by the Grace of God, of the United Kingdom of Great Britain and Northern Ireland, and of her other realms and territories Queen, Head of the Commonwealth, Defender of the Faith.

THE QUEEN IS THE FIGUREHEAD at many annual royal ceremonies and services, such as the State Opening of Parliament and the Garter Service. These splendid occasions are enriched by the brilliant heraldic colours of red, gold, silver and blue, found in the royal arms emblazoned on the Heralds' tabards, and echoed in the various Orders of Chivalry.

The royal arms are used in innumerable ways in connection with the general administration and government of the country, including passports, official documents and letters patent, and since 2008 they have appeared on the reverse side of higher-denomination British coinage. They are probably most recognisable to the general public as the mark of recognition on the goods and products of the Royal Warrant Holders Association. Royal warrants are a mark of recognition to individuals or companies who have supplied goods or services for at least five years to senior members of the royal family. There are around 850 royal warrant-holders.

The royal arms (*right*) can be explained as a shield divided into four equal parts. The first and fourth quarters, on a red background, depict three golden lions passant (i.e. walking towards the left-hand side of the shield, with the right forepaw raised), and guardant (with the face turned towards the viewer). The lions have appeared in the royal arms since the reign of King Richard I (Coeur de Lion) 1189–99. The second quarter, on a gold background, shows a red lion rampant (i.e. standing in profile on the left hindleg), within two narrow red border lines decorated with *fleurs-des-lis*. The lion rampant has been part of the royal arms of Scotland since the time of Alexander II 1214–49. The third quarter, on a blue background, depicts a golden harp with silver strings, representing Ireland. Wales is not represented because it is a principality. Scottish usage shows the royal arms with the Lion of Scotland in the 1st and 4th quarters.

Above the shield is the royal helmet, symbolising the monarch's role as protector, with mantling to represent the slashed cloth which adorns the helmets of kings and princes in battle. Over the helmet is the royal crown, in gold, upon which stands a lion royally crowned. The creatures on either side of the shield (the supporters) are the lion of England and the unicorn from the arms of King James VI of Scotland. The coat of arms features both the motto of English monarchs, *Dieu et mon droit* (God and my right), and the motto of the Order of the Garter, *Honi soit qui mal y pense* (*see caption, right*) on a representation of the Garter behind the shield.

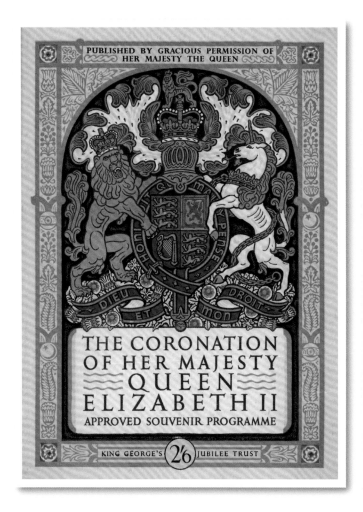

Opposite: The royal cypher is the sovereign's personal device or 'monogram', impressed on all royal and state documents, and used by government departments. It is emblazoned upon the tunics of the Royal Body Guard of the Yeomen of the Guard, the Yeomen Warders of the Tower of London, and may also be seen on some old coins, pillar boxes and Royal Mail vans. A distinction should be made, however, between the Queen's 'personal' cypher and the simpler, more workaday 'public' initials, the former being the sovereign's own monogram and the latter simply a means of identifying a reign.

Above: The royal coat of arms adorns a souvenir programme for the Queen's coronation in 1953. A banner of the arms, the Royal Standard, is flown from royal palaces and residences when the Queen is in residence, and from public buildings only when the Queen is present.

Above: One of the most spectacular of royal ceremonies is the Garter Service, held every year at Windsor Castle. The Order of the Garter is the oldest and most prestigious of all the Orders of Chivalry, founded by King Edward III in 1348. The number is limited to 24 knights (plus royal knights). The badge of the Order, worn on the left shoulder, is a St. George's Cross within the Garter surrounded by radiating silver beams. The emblem of the Order is a blue garter, worn by men on the left knee and by ladies on the left arm, and bearing the famous legend '*Honi soit qui mal y pense*' ('Shame on him who thinks this is evil').

THE EARLY YEARS

From her birth in 1926, Princess Elizabeth was the focus of intense public attention. When she was only three she made the cover of Time *magazine, and her yellow outfit spawned countless imitations. The abdication of her uncle, Edward VIII, was a momentous event; it was to transform the lives of the royal family and recast her destiny. One day she would be Queen. Elizabeth's life was protected and circumscribed, as well as being privileged. Yet she joined the ranks of the ATC in the closing year of the war, and fell in love with the man who was to become her husband, Prince Philip of Greece, when she was just 13 years old.*

LILIBET

Third in line to the British throne

"It almost frightens me that the people should love her so much. I suppose that is a good thing, and I hope that she will be worthy of it, poor little darling."
Elizabeth, Duchess of York

PRINCESS ELIZABETH ALEXANDRA MARY of York was born in her parents' London house, in Bruton Street, Mayfair, on 21 April 1926. Her father, 'Bertie', the Duke of York, and her mother, Elizabeth Bowes-Lyon had been married for three years. As the second son of King George V, Bertie did not expect to become king. Elizabeth was born into a traditional world of wealth and privilege, in a hierarchical household with a full retinue of butlers, footmen, housekeepers and housemaids.

Elizabeth was christened by the Archbishop of Canterbury in a private chapel in Buckingham Palace, wearing a Honiton lace and satin christening robe that had been made for Queen Victoria's eldest daughter and was worn by all subsequent royal children. Her godparents were the Duke of Connaught, the King and Queen, the Princess Royal, her maternal aunt Lady Elphinstone and her grandmother Lady Strathmore.

Elizabeth's early life centred on the nursery, where she was looked after by her nurse, Clara Knight, nicknamed 'Allah', who had also looked after her own mother. It was a life of strict routines, from her morning breakfast to her afternoon walk in a perambulator in Hamilton Place, adjacent to her home, where the young princess was an object of great interest to the public. At the age of nine months, she was left behind in London when her mother and father went on an official tour of Australia and New Zealand. They were away for six months, and Elizabeth spent her time with her doting paternal grandparents. George V, who had been an austere and disciplinarian father, was captivated by his granddaughter.

Elizabeth made her first public appearance at the age of a year and two months, when she was held up to the admiring public on the balcony of Buckingham Palace by her parents, who had just returned from Australia. Shortly afterwards the family moved to 145 Piccadilly, a substantial house with 25 bedrooms, a ballroom, library and conservatory, on the north side of Piccadilly, overlooking Green Park. The nursery floor on the top of the house was occupied by Elizabeth (known as Lilibet), Allah and a new nursery maid, a Scottish girl named Margaret MacDonald, who was nicknamed 'Bobo'.

On her fourth birthday, George V gave Elizabeth her first pony, launching her life-long love of horses. Later that year, Elizabeth's younger sister, Margaret Rose, was born. With no son and heir, it was becoming apparent that Elizabeth was the probable heir to the British throne. Public interest in the young princess was gaining momentum.

A LIFE APART
The protected family life of a princess

> "She is a character. She has an air
> of authority and reflectiveness
> astonishing in an infant."
> *Winston Churchill*

ELIZABETH SOON BECAME a responsible and protective sister to her volatile and mischievous younger sister, Margaret Rose. Her patience and tolerance was rewarded with Princess Margaret's undying loyalty. As the two girls grew older, they were always dressed in matching outfits, and were constantly in each other's company, experiencing the protected, rarified and sequestered lives of young royals.

The arrival of Margaret Rose led to the appointment of Marion Crawford ('Crawfie') as governess to the two young princesses. They followed a schoolroom timetable that would have been recognisable to young ladies of the 19th century: arithmetic, grammar, writing, history, geography. Other ladylike accomplishments included music, art and dancing. In addition the girls were taught French conversation by Madame Montaudon-Smith.

In 1931 King George V gave the family a country estate of their own, the Royal Lodge in Windsor Great Park. This secluded residence was set in substantial gardens, which were enthusiastically tended by the Duke of York. The family enjoyed weekends down at the Lodge, and Elizabeth was given riding lessons by the groom there. In 1932 the people of Wales had presented Elizabeth with a miniature cottage, fully equipped with gadgets and household essentials, and the two princesses enjoyed playing at imaginary housewives. They spent Easter with the King and Queen at Windsor Castle, Christmas and New Year at Sandringham, and in August and September they went up to Scotland to spend time with their maternal grandparents.

The young princesses spent a great deal of their time in adult company, and were very close to both their parents. They had very little contact with other children and were fascinated by them. Crawfie attempted to take them on forays into the outside world, to a museum or art gallery, but they were always recognised and the expeditions were curtailed. They did, however, socialise to a limited extent with children from court circles, and there were frequent children's parties.

While Elizabeth enjoyed playing with her irascible grandfather George V, both sisters were intimidated and awed by their majestic grandmother, Queen Mary. Swathed in fox furs and jewel-bedecked, Queen Mary was profoundly aware of her obligations as a monarch, and a fount of knowledge about the royal family. She inculcated the young Elizabeth with a sense of duty and an awareness of the dignity of the monarchy.

Top left: Princess Elizabeth is photographed, in 1932, in a ballet outfit. Dancing was a required accomplishment of an aristocratic young girl. To this day the Queen is known to be enthusiastic about Scottish country dancing.

Above: The Duchess of York poses with her two daughters, Princess Elizabeth, left, and Princess Margaret, in June 1936 in the garden of the Royal Lodge at Windsor. George V, Elizabeth's beloved grandfather, had died earlier that year, but she was unaware of the impending abdication crisis, which would have a dramatic impact on all their lives.

Above: The Duke of York and Princess Elizabeth sit on a bench with their corgi dogs in the grounds of their London home, 145 Piccadilly. The Yorks had always been fond of dogs, initially labradors. In 1933 the Duke bought his daughters their first corgi, known as Dookie. He was prone to snapping and not very popular in the household, but was soon joined by a partner named Jane, and a royal dynasty of corgis was founded.

Newspaper photographs of the family relaxing together and playing with their dogs were an innovation. Traditional royal photographs were stiff and posed, showing serried ranks of unsmiling members of the royal family, in imposing regalia.

KING GEORGE VI'S CORONATION
A father crowned King

SOUVENIR of the CORONATION of KING GEORGE VI & QUEEN ELIZABETH

Left: A coronation postcard showing George VI, Queen Elizabeth and the two princesses. Souvenirs had originally been made for the planned coronation of Edward VIII. After his abdication they were pulled from the shelves, and manufacturers and designers rushed to make the usual array of stamps, mugs and commemorative coins.

Right: King George VI looks regal in the Imperial State Crown, remade for the coronation from the old Imperial Crown and set with over 3,000 gems. The specially made Queen Consort's crown is a magnificent setting for the famous Koh-i-Noor diamond. The King requested that special lightweight coronets should be made for his young daughters.

THE PROCLAMATION OF ELIZABETH'S Uncle David as new king (Edward VIII), following the death of George V in 1936, was witnessed by his mistress, the American divorcee Wallis Simpson. Edward's infatuation with Mrs Simpson was to change Elizabeth's destiny. Divorce was a taboo at the time and the royal family believed that Edward should put his duty to his kingdom before his private happiness, but he chose the latter, signing the Instrument of Abdication in December 1936.

Elizabeth's father Bertie was to be transformed into George VI. A shy, private man, who had suffered from a severe stammer since childhood, he regarded the prospect with shock and dismay. The royal family's cosy domestic world was turned upside down when they moved to Buckingham Palace in February 1937.

On 12 May 1937 the young princesses, dressed in identical dresses of white lace with trains of purple, ermine-trimmed velvet, witnessed their parents' coronation. From their journey to the Abbey in the Irish state coach, through the lengthy ceremony in which their parents were anointed and enthroned, to their return to the Palace and appearance, in full regalia, on the balcony, the pageant lasted 14 hours.

The coronation is a spectacular and mystical ceremony in which the new monarch is presented to his people (the recognition) and enthroned.

Other integral parts of the rite are the administration of the oath, the anointing with consecrated oil, the vesting with the coronation vestments, and the delivery of the regalia, culminating with the actual crowning, and closed by the reception of Holy Communion.

HOBBIES AND PURSUITS
An exceptional childhood

LIFE IN BUCKINGHAM PALACE was dominated by the business of state, pomp and ceremony. A huge household staff and over 400 servants catered to the needs of the royal family. Against this extraordinary background the King strove to make life as ordinary as possible for his two daughters.

The formation of the 1st Buckingham Palace Company of Girl Guides was intended to compensate for Elizabeth not atttending a normal school. She would meet and play with other children, albeit the daughters of aristocrats and courtiers. Her fellow Girl Guides were expected to curtsey to the Princess, so any notion of democracy was illusory. The Guides met weekly, and their activities all took place in the Palace gardens, George V's summerhouse, or the Palace swimming pool. The highlight was weekends spent with Guides in Windsor Great Park, where they went on treks, camped overnight, built campfires and ate grilled sausages.

Family holidays had to take place in the privacy of the royal estates. Even before her father had become King, the young princesses's first seaside holiday to Eastbourne had been blighted by private detectives and curious crowds. So, for two months every year, in August and September, the royal family escaped the pomp and circumstance of Buckingham Palace for a holiday in Balmoral. They all came to love the peace and quiet of the Scottish estate, and while their parents enjoyed the traditional pleasures of shooting and fishing, the princesses enjoyed the freedom of the outdoors and an endless round of picnics. The children of estate workers and household staff also spent their summers there, and Elizabeth and her friends started their own magazine, *The Snapdragon*. Elizabeth contributed an article to the magazine in which she described the experience of watching the changing of the guard from her window at the Palace.

Elizabeth's passion for horses dated back to her infancy at 145 Piccadilly, when she used to ride her toy horses up and down the nursery corridor. She had learnt to ride at the age of four, and owed her love of horses to the influence of her grandfather, George V. During her teenage years at Windsor she had twice-weekly riding lessons, was taught to jump, and mastered the difficult art of riding sidesaddle.

Despite the glamour of Palace life, the teenage Elizabeth was a countrywoman at heart. Before her royal fate had been decreed, she told Crawfie that she would marry a farmer and have "lots of cows, horses and dogs and children".

Above: Princess Elizabeth, swimming the breaststroke, won the Challenge Shield in the Children's Annual Swimming Meeting at the London Bath Club, when she was 13 years old.

Above right: Princess Elizabeth writes a message to Chief Guide Lady Olave Baden-Powell as her younger sister Princess Margaret Rose looks on, 20 February 1943. They are preparing to send the message (on the occasion of the birthday of Baden-Powell's late husband) by carrier pigeon. The 1st Buckingham Palace Guide Company was formed in 1937 when Princess Elizabeth enrolled as a Girl Guide. The pack included some 20 Guides and 14 Brownies, all children of royal household members and Palace employees. They made their headquarters in a summerhouse in the garden but, with the outbreak of the Second World War, the Company was closed down, and moved to the rural safety of Windsor Castle. Among the badges Princess Elizabeth earned were Cook, Child Nurse, Needlewoman, and Interpreter. In 1943, she became a Sea Ranger; she passed her Boating Permit Test and served as a coxswain. On her 18th birthday the Girl Guide Association presented her with a camping set. In 1946 Elizabeth became Chief Ranger of the British Empire.

A TEENAGE PRINCESS

An eye to the future...

"She is quite serious and with a great deal of character and personality. She asked me a number of questions about life in the United States and they were very serious questions."
Eleanor Roosevelt on meeting Princess Elizabeth

THE KING BEGAN to train his eldest daughter for the day when she would inevitably become Queen. Her schoolroom education syllabus was expanded to include Latin, constitutional history and law, and she was taught by her father and Henry Marten, the Vice-Provost of Eton. She was also instructed in religion by the Archbishop of Canterbury. She was encouraged to take an interest in politics and current affairs, and a visiting ambassador observed, "The King would also talk to his elder daugher more seriously than most fathers do to so young a child. It was as if he spoke to an equal..."

At the age of just 13, Elizabeth met the man she was going to marry. This historic encounter occurred at the Royal Naval College, Dartmouth in the summer of 1939. The King, a graduate of the College, took his wife, daughters and Lord Mountbatten on a tour of the College, and the two girls were placed in the care of their third cousin, an 18-year-old naval cadet named Prince Philip. The young prince was tall, handsome, blue-eyed and athletic and Elizabeth was smitten.

When war broke out, the royal family was at Balmoral, and the princesses remained there for the the first few months of the war. Here, they carried on their usual round of lessons but also participated in weekly sewing parties for war work, which were attended by the local crofters' wives and palace employees. They joined their parents in Sandringham, as usual, for Christmas, and then were sent to the comparative safety of Windsor, where they were to spend the next five years. Their parents' refusal to leave Buckingham Palace, particularly during the Blitz, when the Palace was hit by bombs nine times, won them universal admiration.

At Windsor the teenage Elizabeth lived in the nursery quarters in Augusta Tower, and followed a strict, and timeless, routine: lessons in the morning, a ride in the park before lunch, more lessons in the afternoon, tea, free time (often spent with the Girl Guides), supper and bed. Henry Marten drove up regularly from Eton in a book-laden dogcart to carry on Elizabeth's education in English history. In 1942 Mme Antoinette de Bellaigue, a Belgian aristocrat who escaped occupied Europe, joined the household, and taught the princesses French conversation and continental history.

Elizabeth's future was always in her parents' minds. When important politicians and statesmen joined the King and Queen for lunch, she was summoned to attend, and was encouraged to make conversation with their illustrious guests.

Christmases during the war years in Windsor were always marked by a pantomime, in which the young princesses took part. They were written by the local headmaster, Hubert Tannar, and schoolchildren provided a supporting cast. To set the scene, the paintings that adorned the walls of the Waterloo Chamber were removed from their gilt frames and in their place were inserted bold paintings of pantomime characters. In 1944 music was provided by the Royal Horse Guards, and scenery was designed by the Academy Award winning art director Vincent Korda.

The first pantomime, in 1941, was *Cinderella*; in subsequent years there were peformances of *The Sleeping Beauty*, *Aladdin* and *Old Mother Red Riding Boots*. The 17-year-old Princess Elizabeth can be seen (above left) in the 1943 production of *Aladdin*, with Princess Margaret on the right. To the left, she appears as Aladdin, the starring 'principal boy' role. Prince Philip visited Windsor that Christmas, and would have witnessed her performance.

The money raised from the admission charge went to the Wool Fund, which supplied the wool for comforters for the armed forces.

THE WAR YEARS
Princess and Second Subaltern

WARTIME WINDSOR was austere: chandeliers were taken down, priceless art removed from the walls, the grand state apartments were swathed in dust sheets. Fuel rationing, from 1941, put an end to central heating, and the imposing rooms were heated by coal fires. Hot water was severely rationed. Following the nationwide appeal to 'Dig for Victory', the ornamental gardens were ploughed up and given over to vegetable cultivation. A herd of pigs, fattened on the scraps from the Castle kitchens, supplemented the otherwise monotonous diet.

The Princesses collected tinfoil, rolled bandages and knitted socks for the forces. They contributed pocket money to various charities engaged in war work. A number of charity galas were also staged at Windsor. At one of these galas Elizabeth appeared as a solo artiste, dancing a French minuet to the accompaniment of a violin.

A Company of Grenadier Guards was stationed at Windsor Castle for the duration of the war to guard the royal family. Young officers were invited to lunch at the Castle with the princesses and their governesses, and there were picnics, dances, and games of after-dinner charades.

In 1942, on her 16th birthday, Elizabeth was created a Colonel of the Grenadier Guards, and on the morning of her birthday she inspected the regiment on parade for the very first time. She was also registered at the local Labour Exchange under the wartime youth service scheme. But this proved to be a symbolic gesture; the King was unwilling to let his daughter venture beyond the Castle walls. At 18 she was appointed a Counsellor of State – certain powers could be delegated to her when the King was absent or abroad. But she still felt frustrated: "I ought to do as other girls do."

Finally, in the spring of 1945, Elizabeth was allowed to join the Auxiliary Territorial Service (ATS) as Second Subaltern Elizabeth Alexandra Mary Windsor. She had already been taught to drive in the grounds of Windsor Castle, and on 23 March she embarked on a Cadre Course at Camberley in Surrey. Over the three-week course she mixed, to a limited extent, with ordinary young women, and was given a crash course in car mechanics and map-reading. In July 1945 she was promoted to the rank of Junior Commander. On VE Day, 7 May 1945, she and her sister slipped out, incognito, amongst celebrating London crowds: "I remember lines of unknown people linking arms and walking down Whitehall, all of us just swept along on a tide of happiness and relief."

Top left: Princess Elizabeth, watched by her sister, makes a broadcast to the children of the Empire on 13 October 1940, at the height of the Blitz: "We know, every one of us, that in the end all will be well; for God will care for us and give us victory and peace. And when peace comes, remember it will be for us, the children of today, to make the world of tomorrow a better and happier place."

Above: As No. 230873 Second Subaltern in the ATS Elizabeth enjoyed getting her hands dirty and learnt how to strip, service and maintain an engine.

To pass their final exam, ATS students were expected to drive a truck from their camp to central London. The King and Queen, in consultation with the Home Secretary, agreed that this was too big a risk, only to be greeted by Elizabeth driving a large truck through the Palace gates. She had already made the journey from Camberley to London, through heavy traffic and on her own, because she wanted to attend a party at Buckingham Palace.

Above: On 6 July 1944, Princess Elizabeth, accompanied by her mother, father and Lieutenant General James Doolittle, the 8th Air Force Commander, christened a B17 Flying Fortress 'Rose of York'. On 2 February 1945 the plane was last seen leaving the continent with two engines out and losing height; it was presumed that the North Sea claimed her.

IN LOVE

A new era begins…

Prince Philip of Greece, later the Duke of Edinburgh, enjoys assisting Princess Elizabeth with her coat as she arrives, with Princess Margaret, at Romsey Abbey, Hampshire for the wedding of his cousin Patricia Mountbatten to John Knatchbull in 1946. With a bevy of royal bridesmaids, this was the society wedding of the year.

Philip and Elizabeth were photographed the day after the announcement of their engagement on 10 July 1947 as they strolled arm in arm across the terrace at the Palace. In the words of the Queen: "We feel very happy about it, as he is a very nice person and they have known each other for some years which is a great comfort."

PRINCE PHILIP OF GREECE, the handsome naval cadet whom Elizabeth had met just before the outbreak of war had never been forgotten. Philip had seen active service in the Royal Navy during the war, and when he was on home leave he was a frequent visitor at Windsor Castle, where the romance blossomed. At the end of the war Philip was on duty in the Far East, and did not return to England until March 1946. But Elizabeth's feelings were unchanged; when he proposed to her at Balmoral in late summer 1946 she accepted.

The King was taken aback by his eldest daughter's determination to marry, and asked her to promise that nothing would be made official until her 21st birthday. In the meantime, the family was committed to an official tour of South Africa, which took place in February 1947. Throughout the tour Princess Elizabeth stayed in constant touch with her fiancé, who had become a naturalised British subject, and was now known as Lieutenant Philip Mountbatten. The King could hold out no longer, and on 10 July 1947, "with greatest pleasure", the engagement was announced. That evening the Princess and her fiancé made an impromptu balcony appearance in front of cheering crowds, who relished the prospect of a royal wedding.

Princess Elizabeth and Prince Philip are both great-great-grandchildren of Queen Victoria, Philip through his mother Princess Alice of Battenberg. They are therefore third cousins.

They are also second cousins once removed; Elizabeth's great-great-grandfather was Christian IX of Denmark, whose daughter Alexandra married King Edward VII. Philip was a great-grandson of Christian IX, through his father Prince Andrew of Greece.

A Ceremonial Life

The Queen has lived her entire life in the public eye, but that scrutiny is particularly acute when she is conducting her ceremonial duties. The subject of millions of photographs and many hours of television footage, the Queen has had to share the most intense personal moments of her life, marriages and funerals, with millions of onlookers. She has also been the main player, sometimes crowned, robed and carrying a sceptre, in the drama, ritual and symbolism of a range of ceremonial state occasions, most notably her own coronation, but also the Opening of Parliament, trooping the colour and investitures.

THE WEDDING
A national celebration

IN THE DARK AND GLOOMY DAYS following the end of the Second World War, the wedding of Princess Elizabeth to Lieutenant Philip Mountbatten on 20 November 1947 provided a glimpse of glamour. The notion of a post-war Renaissance was consciously echoed by the designer, Norman Hartnell, who created an exquisite wedding dress inspired by Botticelli's *Primavera*. The white satin gown was garlanded with York roses, star flowers and orange blossom, all encrusted with pearls and crystals.

The morning of the wedding was grey and dismal. There were last minute panics as the Princess made her preparations: her diamond tiara snapped and had to be hastily repaired, and the double string of pearls she intended to wear had to be fetched at the last moment from St. James's Palace. Yet the bride looked serene as she stepped into the Irish state coach with a Sovereign's Escort of the Household Cavalry for her journey to Westminster Abbey.

Accompanied by eight bridesmaids and two pageboys, Elizabeth was greeted by a fanfare, and began her long walk down the nave to the sound of the choir singing 'Praise my Soul, the King of Heaven'. At the altar stood the groom dressed in his ordinary naval uniform, but wearing the insignia of a Knight Companion of the Order of the Garter. Just that morning the King had given him the title of Duke of Edinburgh. The Archbishop of York, who gave the address, told the couple: "Notwithstanding the splendour and national significance of the service in this Abbey, it is in all essentials the same as it would be for any cottager who might be married this afternoon in some small country church."

Princess Elizabeth and the Duke of Edinburgh walked out of the West Door of the Abbey to the accompaniment of Mendelssohn's *Wedding March*. They travelled through the crowded and drizzly streets of London in the Glass Coach, with its scarlet-liveried outriders and Household Cavalry escort, followed by the King and Queen Elizabeth, Queen Mary and Princess Andrew of Greece (Philip's mother) and some 30 foreign royal guests – a colourful parade that thrilled the waiting crowds.

After the requisite balcony appearance a wedding breakfast was held for 150 guests, with a menu featuring unrationed partridges and Filet de Sole Mountbatten. After the reception the couple were showered with rose petals by their family, and drove in an open carriage to Waterloo Station, beginning their honeymoon at Broadlands in Hampshire.

THE WEDDING
Presents fit for a Princess

Despite the austerity of post-war Britain, Princess Elizabeth's wedding was marked by a huge outpouring of public affection, both at home and abroad. The young couple were showered with gifts, and when the news came out that the Princess would have to collect clothing coupons for her dress, she was inundated with gifts of coupons (which had to be returned).

The presents had been arriving for weeks before the wedding, but it was not until the 17th and 18th November that those who had given presents were invited to St. James's Palace to see them. The gifts from the royal family were given pride of place in the Throne Room. The King and Queen had given their daughter a necklace of diamond and rubies and two strings of pearls. Queen Mary's presents to her granddaughter included a diamond tiara, diamond earrings and a diamond brooch. Princess Margaret, on a more practical note, gave her sister a cream plastic picnic set and some table glassware.

The enormous variety of the presents betrayed their provenance: from the Aga Khan's gift of a chestnut filly and a set of Dresden porcelain from the Vatican to hand-knitted jumpers, embroidered samplers and home-made tea cosies. Appropriately enough, for the wedding of a future head of the Commonwealth, there were countless gifts from abroad: a hunting lodge from the people of Kenya, a mink coat from Canada, a fur wrap from Newfoundland, a gold salver from Australia, a writing desk from New Zealand. Mahatma Gandhi presented the Princess with a hand-woven tray cloth; Queen Mary, under the mistaken impression that it was a loincloth, commented "Such an indelicate gift... what a horrible thing."

Some of the presents were practical items for a young couple setting up home in straitened times: including a vacuum cleaner, a fridge, a sewing machine and even wallpaper. One lady from Brooklyn sent the couple the gift of a turkey – she was worried that food shortages in England were even having an impact on the royal family. At the Princess's request some of the wedding presents took the form of hospital endowments and subscriptions to charity.

The couple's wedding cake, nine feet high and constructed of four tiers, was created with the intention of reaching out to the Commonwealth, and as such used ingredients from around the world, including some given by the Australian Girl Guides. After the wedding, slices of cake were distributed all over the country.

Far left: Three girls representing the armed forces admiring the tea and coffee service which is a wedding present from the National Association of Training Corps to Princess Elizabeth. The girls were chosen to deliver the service to St. James's Palace.

Left: A gift of ingredients for Princess Elizabeth's wedding cake from the Australian Girl Guides is presented at Guide headquarters in London. Food was rationed in post-war Australia, but the authorities took sugar and butter 'off-ration' when they heard of the Girl Guides' plan.

Left: Mr Leslie W. Lang displays a photograph of a painting he sent as a wedding gift to Princess Elizabeth. He is queuing, with other members of the public, to see the 2,500 wedding presents on display on 18 November 1947. This was an occasion when ordinary people could rub shoulders with dignitaries and grandees, and they dressed formally for this exceptional visit to a royal palace.

THE CORONATION
Symbolic splendour

Six maids of honour attended Elizabeth throughout the coronation, and were responsible for carrying her train. The Mistress of the Robes, the Dowager Duchess of Devonshire, seen standing beside the Queen, prepared the Queen for her anointing. The maids of honour wore Hartnell-designed dresses of white satin with a gold motif.

Right: The Queen in her coronation regalia, photographed by Cecil Beaton.

ELIZABETH'S CORONATION TOOK PLACE some 15 months after her accession, which followed her father's death, aged 56. Her coronation, on 2 June 1953, with its ancient pageantry, ceremonial and mystical rituals, was freighted with symbolic significance.

On her accession, Elizabeth had dedicated herself to service of the Commonwealth. Her embroidered white satin gown, designed by Norman Hartnell, used subtle shades of pink, blue, yellow and green to incorporate the emblems of Britain and the Commonwealth into the design: the Tudor rose, the thistle, leek, shamrock, the Canadian maple leaf, the Australian wattle flower, the fern of New Zealand, the protea of South Africa, the wheat and jute of Pakistan and the lotus of Ceylon. Made of Lullingstone silk, it was worked by six embroideresses in the utmost secrecy.

Before the coronation, the Queen practised for hours wearing the 5-lb St. Edward's Crown. On her way to the Abbey she wore the ermine-edged Robe of State of Crimson Velvet. On her return she wore the Imperial Robe of Purple Velvet, lined with white silk and ermine-edged. Both robes, made by Ede and Ravenscroft, were cut on narrower than traditional lines to reduce the weight and display the magnificent gown.

"Will you solemnly promise and swear to govern the Peoples of the United Kingdom of Great Britain and Northern Ireland… and of your Possessions and other territories to any of them belonging or pertaining, according to their respective laws and customs?

Will you to your utmost power maintain the Laws of God and the true profession of the Gospel?…"

"The things which I have here before promised, I will perform and keep."

THE CORONATION
An ancient ritual

CORONATION DAY, 2 June 1953, was grey, cool and drizzly. But the streets of London were crowded with millions of onlookers, who gazed at the stately procession of royalty, peers, ambassadors, diplomats and dignitaries, who arrived at Westminster Abbey in an array of cars and carriages.

The guests began taking their seats from 7am, with the royal family arriving last in strict order of precedence: the Duchess of Kent with her children, the Duchess of Gloucester with her two sons, the Princess Royal, Princess Margaret and, finally, the Queen Mother. At 11.20am the Queen arrived at the Abbey in the state coach, and was greeted by the Duke of Norfolk, Earl Marshal. She was accompanied by Prince Philip, resplendent in the uniform of an Admiral of the Fleet, with gold bullion epaulettes and Garter Star.

The ensuing ceremony was a piece of theatre that had been six months in the making. The Abbey had been closed since January so that tiered seating could be built for the 8,251 guests. Acres of blue and gold carpet had been woven in Glasgow. In Bradford 4,000 yards of velvet had been woven to cover 2,000 chairs and 5,700 stools. The 60-strong orchestra and 400-strong choir had rehearsed relentlessly.

The Queen walked down the aisle to the strains of Parry's 'I was Glad', and shouts of 'Vivat Regina'. The ensuing ceremony has remained fundamentally unchanged over the last thousand years; the first English monarch to be crowned in the Abbey was William the Conqueror in 1066. It is steeped in symbolism, pageantry and a religious sense of awe. It brings together not only the monarch, but the greatest religous leaders in the realm and the scions of the nobility.

The core of the ceremony, performed by the Archbishop of Canterbury, was the recognition of the sovereign by the assembled congregation, the administration of the Coronation Oath, the anointing with holy oil (the secret recipe contains oils of orange flowers, roses, jasmine, cinnamon, musk, civet and ambergris), the investiture with the royal regalia and the actual crowning. These key moments in the historic service were punctuated with trumpet fanfares and shouts of 'God save the Queen', and the robing in ritual garments – a simple white over-dress, the golden supertunic and the Dalmatic Robe. The St. Edward's Crown, made for the coronation of Charles II, was placed on the Queen's head at 12.34pm, and the acclamation of the congregation was matched by the firing of canon salutes from the Tower of London. Elizabeth exited the Abbey at 2.53pm, wearing the Imperial State Crown.

Far left: The Queen and Prince Philip were conveyed to and from Westminster Abbey in the Gold State Coach. The coach was first used, by George III, in 1762. The 24-ft long coach is bedecked with a wealth of symbols, including tritons, tridents, and three cherubs, representing England, Scotland and Ireland and carrying the Sceptre, Sword of State and Ensign of Knighthood.

Left: The Queen sits in St. Edward's Chair, made on the orders of Edward I in 1300. She wears the St. Edward's Crown and holds the Sceptre with the Cross ('the Ensign of power and justice') and the Rod with the Dove (representing equity and mercy). She has also been presented with the Sword and the Armills (bracelets) of sincerity and wisdom. The Dalmatic robe represents righteousness. At the moment of crowning, in a supremely dramatic climax, the Princes and Princesses of the Blood and peers and peeresses put on their own coronets to repeated shouts of 'God save the Queen'.

THE CORONATION
The people's Queen

ALL ASPECTS OF THE CORONATION were overseen by the Coronation Commission, nominated by Elizabeth, with the Duke of Edinburgh as Chairman and the Duke of Norfolk as Vice-Chairman. One of their first decisions, approved by the Cabinet, was that no television cameras would be allowed in the Abbey for the service; instead the public would have to be satisfied with a 'cinematographic film' of proceedings. This attempt to preserve the ancient mystique of the monarchy caused a public uproar. A compromise was proposed: the public would see the recognition, crowning and homage, but the most sacred parts of the ceremony – the anointing and communion – would remain private. In the event over 20 million people watched the BBC coverage of the coronation, and many more watched worldwide.

Britain was still plunged in post-war austerity, and the coronation was the excuse for a nationwide party. Although rationing was still in force, Churchill insisted that an extra 1lb of sugar should be made available to everybody. Rationing restrictions were lifted from eggs and sweets. Even applications to roast a whole ox, a traditional coronation celebration, were allowed under certain circumstances. The Government spent over £2 million on celebrations.

London was *en fête*. Stands for spectators were constructed all along The Mall, which was adorned with triumphal arches and vast metalwork crowns. It is estimated that 3 million people lined the ceremonial route on Coronation Day. From very early in the morning they were able to observe a parade of cloaked peers, peeresses in evening dress, and foreign royalty in an array of national costumes. When the ceremonial in Westminster Abbey was finished, the newly crowned Queen was paraded through the streets of London. A cavalcade of coaches, with mounted escorts, wound their way to Trafalgar Square, St. James's Street, Piccadilly, through Hyde Park, along Oxford Street and Regent Street and along The Mall. Six hours and twenty minutes after she had set out, the Queen returned to Buckingham Palace. She appeared on the balcony, to ecstatic shouts from the crowds, wearing the magnificent Imperial State Crown.

The RAF marked the occasion with a flypast down The Mall and Victoria Embankment was lit up with a magnificent firework display. All over the country there were street parties, village fêtes, bonfires and services of commemoration. Constance Spry devised a special dish, Coronation Chicken, for the coronation lunch for 350 foreign guests, and this reminder of the big day has remained enduringly popular.

Opposite left: The Tivoli Cinema in the Strand, London, advertises a full length technicolour film of the coronation of Queen Elizabeth II. Many people acquired televisions especially for the coronation; others had to make do with newsreel footage and documentary features.

Above left: A line of movie cameras and tripods is set up for the coronation. While some traditionalists felt it was wrong for people to watch such a solemn occasion while drinking tea in their front rooms, the wishes of the people prevailed – it marked the beginning of the television age.

Above: Spectators in dense crowds got a clear view of the coronation procession by investing in commemorative 'Coronation Copescopes' (folding periscopes), made of printed card with twin glass mirrors. These were produced as a souvenir of the coronation of Queen Elizabeth II.

Left: The bunting is out for a coronation street party in Morpeth Street, in London's East End. The tradition of holding street parties dates to the celebration of the Armistice after the First World War. The coronation was seen as a great excuse for a party, and many thousands of parties were held.

ROYAL WEDDINGS
Public jubilation

The Queen Mother and Queen, both magnificent in full court dress, and Prince Charles, in ruffled cravat and kilt, at the wedding of Princess Margaret in 1960. Both Elizabeth and her mother were delighted with the marriage, despite many courtiers' misgivings that Margaret's royal upbringing would not sit comfortably with Antony Armstrong-Jones's more bohemian lifestyle.

THE QUEEN HAS BEEN a guest at many marriages over her long reign, but it is at the weddings of her close family, especially her own children and grandchildren, that ceremonial is most closely blended with familial pride and affection.

The wedding of her sister Princess Margaret in 1960 was a day of public celebration – there had been enormous sympathy for the Princess when, in 1955, she relinquished her romance with the divorced Group Captain Peter Townsend. It was also a moment of intense personal happiness for the Queen, who was delighted to see her younger sister married to the bohemian photographer, Antony Armstrong-Jones, and clearly very much in love. Princess Margaret's wedding was the last occasion on which the royal guests wore full length dresses, and the Queen was resplendent in turquoise blue silk and lace.

While some of the less important royal families of Europe declined to attend the wedding of Princess Margaret, feeling that the marriage of a royal princess to a 'commoner' was far from acceptable, a precedent had been set and over the next few decades the Queen was to attend a number of royal marriages to a range of non-royal partners, from army and

navy officers and a public relations executive to a rugby professional. In keeping with the times, the royal family has learnt to live with divorce; in 2005 the Queen attended a service of blessing at Windsor Castle after her divorced eldest son married a divorced second wife in a civil ceremony.

The first weddings of her two eldest children, Charles and Anne, and the wedding of the Queen's second son, Andrew, were all grand state occasions in St. Paul's Cathedral and Westminster Abbey. They were the focus of intense public interest, attracting television audiences of up to 750 million worldwide. Prince Edward, perhaps the most publicity-shy of the Queen's children, opted for a quiet wedding in St. George's Chapel, Windsor. The Queen presided at all these occasions, accustomed to seeing her own family's rites of passage becoming acts of theatrical ceremonial, eagerly attended by an enthusiastic public.

In 2011, she watched, resplendent in a striking yellow outfit, as her grandson Prince William, the second in line to the throne, married the girlfriend he met at university, Catherine Middleton. Two months later her eldest granddaughter, Zara Phillips, tied the knot with the rugby player Mike Tindall in a private ceremony at Canongate Kirk in Edinburgh.

Above: The Queen, smartly dressed in a sapphire blue coat and matching hat, waits anxiously for the appearance of the bride, at the wedding of Princess Anne on 14 November 1973. As an increasingly modern monarch, she had played no part in choosing her daughter's husband; the choice of a professional Army officer and fellow horse-enthusiast was Anne's alone. The wedding was watched by 500 million viewers worldwide, while crowds 50,000 strong lined the route to Westminster Abbey. Princess Anne wore the same tiara that her mother had worn on her wedding, on loan from the Queen Mother. Her dress, shimmering with mirror jewels and seed pearls, echoed her own mother's wedding dress.

Above: On the occasion of her son Prince Edward's marriage to PR executive Sophie Rhys-Jones, the Queen chose a full-length lilac silk dress with the pearls and earrings she wore to her own wedding. She is seen here with the father of the bride, tyre sales executive Christopher Rhys-Jones. Prince Edward eschewed the traditional military career of male members of the royal family, resigning his commisison in the Marines after just four months. He also opted for a much more low-key wedding, which took place on 19 June 1999 at St. George's Chapel, Windsor, with a reception at Windsor Castle. Edward toasted "the hostess of this evening – perhaps the most wonderful mother in the world, the Queen."

ROYAL FUNERALS
Public mourning

> "Such sorrow is a very strange experience – it really changes one's whole life, whether for better or worse I don't know yet..."
> *Elizabeth, on the death of her father, King George VI*

THERE CAN BE FEW OCCASIONS when the public face of royalty is more burdensome than at times of family bereavement. The trappings of state funerals create an added weight of solemnity and mourners face intense scrutiny at a time when they crave privacy.

Elizabeth's first experience of royal mourning came with the funeral of her grandfather, King George V. On 27 January 1936 she was taken, dressed in black, to see the lying-in-state of her grandfather at Westminster Hall. She was impressed by the absolute stillness of the King's four sons, as they stood solemn guard at the four corners of the catafalque bearing the coffin, while members of the public filed past. The following day, she watched as the coffin was lowered into the family vault beneath St. George's Chapel, Windsor.

Her own father's death in 1952 precipitated her accession to the Crown. She heard the news while staying in Treetops Hotel, Kenya, and during the long journey back to Britain she managed to hide her grief and remained calm and collected. When her grandmother Queen Mary, a strict adherent of royal protocol, curtsied and kissed the new sovereign's hand, Elizabeth was appalled by the abruptness of the transition. King George VI's lying-in-state was attended by 305,806 people, and after a sombre journey through the streets of London he was interred at Windsor. The Queen sprinkled earth from a silver dish as the words of committal were read.

Elizabeth was to preside over two more family funerals at St. George's Chapel. Fifty years to the day since the burial of King George VI, on 15 February 2002, Princess Margaret's funeral was held at Windsor, though she was not buried there. Just two months later, the Queen Mother was lying in state at Westminster Hall. As the Abbey's Tenor Bell tolled 101 times for each of her 101 years, crowds gathered for the ceremony at Westminster Abbey. Afterwards a million people lined the streets to see the funeral cortège pass on its way to St. George's Chapel, Windsor, for a private interment.

Above left: A sombre Queen Elizabeth II stands in front of her mother's coffin at the funeral service in Westminster Abbey in 2002. It is surmounted by the Queen Mother's platinum crown and draped with her standard.

Right: A black veiled Queen Mother, flanked by her daughter Elizabeth and the Duke of Edinburgh, watches as George VI's coffin is lifted from the train that brought the body from Sandringham to London for his state funeral.

THE STATE OPENING OF PARLIAMENT
The nation's figurehead

The QUEEN *has performed the ceremony in* EVERY YEAR OF HER REIGN *except for 1959 and 1963, when she was pregnant with Princes Andrew and Edward respectively.*

PARLIAMENT'S ANNUAL STATE OPENING takes place every year in the autumn, and additionally after a general election. This is an occasion on which the Queen is called upon to play a central, and majestic, role in a ceremony which is steeped in tradition and makes reference to the sometimes chequered relationship between the monarchy and the House of Commons.

Before the State Opening, the Yeomen of the Guard search the cellars of the Houses of Parliament, a tradition dating back to the Gunpowder Plot of 1605, when Guy Fawkes attempted to blow up Parliament. The Queen is driven in a state carriage from Buckingham Palace to the Palace of Westminster, preceded by the Imperial Crown, which travels in a separate carriage. Preceded by the Sword of State and the Cap of Maintenance, the Queen progresses through Westminster Palace to the House of Lords, wearing her Crown and crimson parliamentary robe.

The official known as Black Rod is then sent to summon the Commons, and in an annual ritual the door to the Chamber is symbolically slammed in his face by the Serjeant at Arms to assert the Commons' independence. The door is opened in response to three knocks with his ebony staff of office. The Speaker and the Serjeant at Arms, with mace in hand, then lead the Prime Minister and Leader of the Opposition with a deliberate lack of haste to the Lords' Chamber. The speech, written by the Prime Minister and Cabinet and setting out plans for the coming Session, is then delivered by the Queen.

The Queen's first State Opening of Parliament was in November 1952. She had acceded to the throne earlier that year, but had not been crowned. Dressed in a gold lace gown and wearing the purple velvet robe worn by the young Queen Victoria, she made a dignified debut, and addressed the nation in 'clear and well-modulated' tones. She was not, however, able to wear the Imperial State Crown, as this is an honour only accorded to the monarch after the coronation.

Above left: The Queen at the State Opening on 29 October 1974 with Prince Philip. The single throne used by Queen Victoria was replaced by a throne for the King and a companion seat for the Queen Consort upon the accession of Edward VII.

Right: The Queen and Prince Philip process through the Royal Gallery in Westminster, on 18 November 2009. It is traditional for a 'hostage' MP, a Government whip, to be held at Buckingham Palace during the Opening to secure the monarch's safe return.

JUBILEES

A shared anniversary

Left: On the occasion of the Golden Jubilee in 2002 Queen Elizabeth and Prince Philip ride in the Golden State Carriage from Buckingham Palace to St. Paul's Cathedral. The 24-foot long, 4-ton coach was commissioned in 1760 for the astronomical sum of £7,562. The heavy coach can only be pulled at a walk by eight horses.

Right: On 7 June 1977 Queen Elizabeth II and Prince Philip are presented to a group of Church Aldermen after the Service of Thanksgiving, attended by 2,700 guests, at St. Paul's Cathedral on the occasion of her Silver Jubilee. More than a million people lined the streets of London to see the Queen.

BONFIRE BEACONS, FIREWORKS, carriage processions, balcony appearances, walkabouts, street parties, flag-waving, flypasts…The traditional celebrations of the milestone years in her long reign have surprised and gratified the Queen, who has been touched by the genuine enthusiasm and fervour displayed by the public.

Her Silver Jubilee, in 1977, came at a time of severe economic recession, and the year-long celebrations did a great deal to dispel that gloom. As well as the traditional service of thanksgiving at St. Paul's, the Queen and Prince Philip toured a total of 36 UK counties over a period of just three months. Over the course of the Jubilee year they embarked on a marathon Commonwealth tour, travelling to the Pacific Islands, New Zealand, Australia, the West Indies and Canada.

The Golden Jubilee in 2002 followed a similar pattern, confounding the gloomy predictions of anti-royalists. Over a million people converged on London for a weekend of concerts at Buckingham Palace and a service of thanksgiving at St. Paul's. The Queen and Prince Philip's tour of the Commonwealth countries during that year covered 40,000 miles, and an ambitious domestic tour took them to 70 towns and cities within the United Kingdom.

"When I was twenty-one I pledged my life to the service of our people and I asked for God's help to make good that vow. Although that vow was made in my salad days, when I was green in judgement, I do not regret nor retract one word of it."
Elizabeth II, on her Silver Jubilee

"Gratitude, respect and pride, these words sum up how I feel about the people of this country and the Commonwealth – and what this Golden Jubilee means to me."
Elizabeth II, on her Golden Jubilee

TROOPING THE COLOUR
A historic spectacle

In 1952 ELIZABETH became the first ENGLISH QUEEN since Elizabeth I (1558–1603) to review her troops on HORSEBACK.

ON THE DEATH OF HER FATHER Elizabeth II became Colonel-in-Chief of all the Guards Regiments and Corps of Royal Engineers, and Captain-General of the Royal Regiment of Artillery and the Honourable Artillery Company. As the sovereign, she is also the head of the Army, Navy and Royal Air Force. Few ceremonies, however, bring home her close relationship to the armed forces so vividly as Trooping the Colour, also known as the Sovereign's Birthday Parade.

This annual event, held every June, dates back to 1755. In a display of perfectly-honed ceremonial it allows the entire Household Division, composed of the Household Cavalry and five regiments of the Guards Division, to salute the sovereign on the occasion of her official birthday.

The Queen first took part in the ceremony, when it was her father who was being honoured, in 1949. As a young girl, she had mastered the difficult art of riding sidesaddle, and for 36 years she appeared, mounted, in the scarlet tunic of the regiment of Guards whose colour was being trooped, a blue riding skirt, riding boots, and a tricorn hat surmounted by the relevant regimental plume. Since 1987 she has attended the ceremony in a carriage.

Over 1,400 officers, 200 horses and 400 musicians are involved in the parade, and the regiments involved take it in turn to troop their 'colour', or regimental standard. This was once a vital battle preparation, ensuring soldiers recognised, and followed, the banner of their own regiment.

The parade route extends from Buckingham Palace along The Mall to Horse Guards Parade, Whitehall and back again. At 11am the Royal Procession arrives and the Queen takes the Royal Salute. The parade begins with the Inspection, the Queen driving slowly down the ranks of all eight Guards and then past the Household Cavalry.

Above: Elizabeth II, flanked by Princess Anne and Prince Philip, enjoys the traditional flypast of RAF planes over Buckingham Palace at the end of the Trooping the Colour in 2008. The connection of Trooping the Colour with flypasts began in 1913 when the Royal Flying Corps Military Wing performed a flypast for King George V.

Right: Princess Elizabeth, riding sidesaddle, represents King George VI at the Trooping the Colour ceremony on 7 June 1951. Her father was too ill to perform many of his public and ceremonial duties, and Elizabeth stepped into the breach. She is riding 'Winston', a magnificent chestnut-brown, who took part in many state duties.

INVESTITURES

Acknowledging and honouring service

Left: The Queen bestows an OBE on the actor Michael Sheen for his services to drama during an investiture at Buckingham Palace in 2009.

Right: The veteran entertainer and television host Bruce Forsyth is knighted by Queen Elizabeth at Buckingham Palace in June 2011.

THE QUEEN IS KNOWN as 'the fount of honour' and, since feudal times, the sovereign has conferred honours on his/her subjects. Today, honours may be awarded for gallantry, courage, outstanding achievement, or service to the community or the Crown. This is the moment when the Queen is able to meet, and congratulate, outstanding members of the public; she regards investitures as the most enjoyable of her ceremonial duties.

Every year the New Year's Honours List and the Birthday Honours List are announced in the *London Gazette*, and summonses are sent to the recipients requesting them to attend an investiture at Buckingham Palace. On average 14 investitures a year are held at Buckingham Palace, and once every five years an investiture is held at the Palace of Holyroodhouse in Scotland; around 2,600 people a year receive their award in person. The Queen or a senior member of the royal family – the Prince of Wales or Princess Royal – officiates. The Queen held her first investiture on 6 February 1952, shortly after her accession.

At Buckingham Palace investitures take place in the Ballroom, and about 135 people are invited to attend to receive their

orders, decorations and medals. At the start of the ceremony the Queen enters the room flanked by two Gurkha orderly officers, a tradition instituted by Queen Victoria. On duty on the dais are five members of The Queen's Body Guard of the Yeomen of the Guard, which was created in 1485 by Henry VII; they are the oldest military corps in the United Kingdom. The Queen herself pins the decoration on the recipients; as each recipient steps up to receive the honour her equerry gives her a brief summary of his/her achievements. Those who are receiving a knighthood kneel on an investiture stool before the Queen and she uses the sword that belonged to her father, King George VI, to dub the knight – a ritual dating back to the Middle Ages.

The most prestigious honour is membership of the Most Noble Order of the Garter, which is restricted to 24 Knights Companion. Every June the Knights gather at Windsor Castle and the Queen invests any new Companions with the insignia (a broad riband worn over the shoulder, a star and a collar) at a Chapter of the Order in the Throne Room of Windsor Castle. This is followed by a luncheon hosted by the Queen and the Duke of Edinburgh and a procession through the wards of Windsor Castle to St. George's Chapel.

FAMILY LIFE

"Like all the best families, we have our share of eccentricities, of impetuous and wayward youngsters and of family disagreements", confessed the Queen in 1989. But despite its inevitable dramas and disappointments, family life has been a source of great pleasure and solace to Her Majesty from earliest childhood, when she was close to her parents and sister, through motherhood to her eventual standing as a wise and revered grandmother and great-grandmother.

DAUGHTER
Reciprocal respect and loyalty

"She had an infectious zest for living, and this remained with her until the very end."
Elizabeth II on her mother

THE HONOURABLE ELIZABETH Angela Marguerite Bowes-Lyon gave birth to the first of her two daughters on 21 April 1926, at her parents' London home, 17 Bruton Street in Mayfair. In doing so, she made Elizabeth the only British monarch to have been born in a house with an ordinary door number.

Joined by a sister, Margaret Rose, in 1930, the young Elizabeth enjoyed a close relationship with her family, always referred to by her father, George VI, as "us four". Her father, whose own upbringing had been austere and regimented, was anxious to create a warm and loving home for his daughters. The princesses were home-educated under the supervision of a governess and their mother who, in spite of her many duties, made time to provide guidance, religious and otherwise, for her daughters.

Elizabeth's cousin Margaret Rhodes described her as "a jolly little girl, but fundamentally sensible and well-behaved". These character traits were to stand her in good stead when fate made her father King and herself heir to the throne, aged just ten. Both parents sought to prepare Elizabeth for her future role, extending her educational syllabus, and ensuring she met many influential people.

During the Second World War Queen Elizabeth declared, on being asked to leave London: "The children won't go without me. I won't leave the King. And the King will never leave." George VI, who had worked hard to overcome his stutter and become the wartime voice of the nation, emerged as a popular national figurehead. He was extremely protective of his elder daughter, resisting her requests to join the armed forces until 1945. His premature death, at the age of just 57 in 1952, was a terrible blow for all his family, and thrust a stoical, but grieving, Elizabeth onto the world stage.

The Queen Mother continued to inspire her eldest daughter by serving her country assiduously and long, remaining involved in public life into very old age. When she passed away, peacefully in her sleep at the Royal Lodge at Windsor at the age of 101, the Queen was at her bedside.

Top left: King George VI relaxes with his daughter during a visit to Natal National Park in South Africa, 1947. This was Elizabeth's first overseas tour, which she made with her parents and her sister.

Right: 14-year-old 'Lilibet' and her mother enjoy an affectionate moment at Windsor, their smiles testament to their fortitude and role as morale-boosters to the public during the Second World War.

SISTER
A dedicated elder sibling

Princess Margaret's DIVORCE *from Antony Armstrong-Jones was the* FIRST DIVORCE *in the royal family since* HENRY VIII's.

BORN FOUR AND A HALF YEARS apart, Elizabeth and her sister Margaret Rose enjoyed a blissful early childhood at the heart of a loving family. Educated at home, the girls' early lives were closeted and cosy, taken up by riding lessons, card games, tea with cousins, and family pillow-fights. All that was to change when their father suddenly became King in 1936. According to the royal biographer Harold Nicolson, 10-year-old Elizabeth raced to the nursery to tell her younger sister, and was greeted by the reply: "Does that mean that you will have to be the next Queen?... Poor you."

Always less conventional and serious than her sibling – both by nature and also because of the lesser responsibilities that awaited her – Margaret was nonetheless deeply loyal to Elizabeth, and missed her sorely when she married, when Margaret was aged 17. However, Margaret was far from inactive when it came to royal duties: she undertook her first solo public engagement aged just 15, when she opened a Save the Children play centre in London, and had 50 engagements in her 'coming out' year, when she was 18.

Despite their loving relationship, the more sensible older sister sometimes had issues with her sister's free-spiritedness, mostly famously when Margaret informed her, as Elizabeth prepared for her coronation, that she wished to marry Peter Townsend, a divorced commoner. Elizabeth, naturally sympathetic to her sister and also – like the Queen Mother – fond of Townsend, a long-standing family friend who had been close to the late King, initially asked Margaret to wait a year. But ulimately the Queen was constrained to follow the advice of the prime minister, Winston Churchill, and the Archbishop of Canterbury, who were both adamant such a union could not go ahead.

After her subsequent marriage to photographer Antony Armstrong-Jones ended in divorce, Margaret spent the rest of her life in an apartment in Kensington Palace and never re-married, but instead spent a great deal of time with the Queen and Queen Mother. When she died aged 71 in 2002, after a period marred by ill health, it was her mother and sister who were the most badly affected.

The former Cabinet minister Lord St. John of Fawsley, a long-time friend of Margaret, commented: "I never in all my life heard Princess Margaret say a harsh or critical word about the Queen. She was totally devoted to her and the Queen will miss her very much."

Top left: Elizabeth and Margaret with the silver cup awarded them at the Royal Windsor Horse Show in 1945, when they won first prize in a driving competition, aged 19 and 14 respectively. The annual show was conceived in 1943 as part of the Wings for Victory Campaign, under their parents' patronage. This was aimed at raising funds for RAF aircraft and Windsor contributed almost £400,000, equivalent to 78 Typhoon aircraft. Since then the horse show has been an annual tourist attraction in Windsor Great Park.

Above: The Queen and her younger sister arrive by carriage at Horseguards Parade in 1993, where the Queen presented new standards to units of the Household Cavalry. The Cavalry, made up of the senior regular regiments in the British Army, with traditions dating from 1660, act as the Queen's personal bodyguard. Princess Margaret was Colonel-in-Chief of a number of military units, including the 15th/19th The King's Royal Hussars and The Royal Highland Fusiliers, and was patron or president of over 80 organisations.

WIFE

A long and happy marriage

> "I, Philip, Duke of Edinburgh, do become your liege man of life and limb, and of earthly worship; and faith and truth I will bear unto you, to live and die, against all manner of folks. So help me God."
> *Prince Philip at the Queen's coronation, 1953*

ELIZABETH II FIRST FELL for her third cousin through Queen Victoria and second cousin through King Christian IX of Denmark when he was assigned to give her and Margaret a tour of the Royal Naval College in Dartmouth in 1939, where Philip was a cadet. Elizabeth was just 13, Philip five years older, but the pair began a correspondence that would culminate in his asking George VI for his daughter's hand in 1946.

The Corfu-born son of Prince Andrew of Greece and Denmark and Princess Alice, Philip had renounced his Greek and Danish royal titles and his allegiance to the Greek Crown, converted from Greek Orthodoxy to Anglicanism, and become a naturalised British subject by the time of their wedding at Westminster Abbey on 20 November 1947. Having taken up residence at Clarence House, they had two children in swift succession – Charles in 1948 and Anne in 1950. The Duke continued with his naval career, and the young family spent a couple of happy years on Malta.

After her accession to the throne, Elizabeth announced that Philip was to have "place, pre-eminence and precedence" next to her "on all occasions and in all meetings, except where otherwise provided by Act of Parliament", in doing so giving him precedence over Prince Charles except in the British Parliament. The Queen has always been strongly supportive of Philip and his endeavours – a fact that she formalised by making him Prince of the United Kingdom in the late 1950s.

Commended for his support of the Queen by the Speaker of the House of Commons during her Golden Jubilee in 2002, the Duke of Edinburgh is the longest-serving royal consort in British history. As well as assisting her in her duties, he has also been patron of about 850 different organisations, ranging from regiments to charities, with the emphasis on the environment, industry, sport, and education. Most famously, the Duke of Edinburgh Award Scheme, founded in 1956 to give young people "a sense of responsibility to themselves and their communities", has had a worldwide impact.

Asked about the secret of their long and happy marriage, Philip has cited the Queen's "quality of tolerance in abundance", while the Queen, in a speech at London's Guildhall on their 50th wedding anniversary in 1997, said: "He has, quite simply, been my strength and stay all these years, and I, and his whole family, and this and many other countries, owe him a debt greater than he would ever claim or we shall ever know."

Far left: Princess Elizabeth and the Duke of Edinburgh attend the Royal Horse Show at Windsor in 1949. The couple has shared a lifelong passion for equestrian sports, with Philip one of Britain's best polo players until his 50s, and in his 60s, a competitor in the world carriage-driving championships — a sport for which he wrote the international rulebook.

Left: The Queen and Prince Philip arrive at St. Paul's Cathedral in high spirits for a service of thanksgiving on the occasion of Her Majesty's 80th birthday in June 2006. The following year the couple went to Westminster Abbey to celebrate their Diamond Anniversary, which marked 60 years of combining their royal duties with their roles as parents to four children and grandparents to many more. Their partnership owes its durability to, more than anything else, mutual support and trust.

MOTHER
to Charles and Anne

"The baby is very sweet, and Philip and I are enormously proud of him. I still find it hard to believe that I really have a baby of my own!"
Queen Elizabeth

ELIZABETH GAVE BIRTH to her first child, Charles, in 1948 when she was aged 22, and her second, Anne, before two years were out. Within three years of Anne's arrival, Elizabeth was crowned Queen. The four-year-old Charles retained vivid memories of his mother's coronation, when he sat between the Queen Mother and his Aunt Margaret before joining his parents and other members of the royal family on the balcony of Buckingham Palace. Charles also remembered his mother in the weeks leading up to the coronation, coming to say goodnight to him and Anne wearing the St. Edward's Crown.

Childhood photos show Charles and Anne playing on the deck of the Royal Yacht *Brittania*, aged five and three, and Charles in a pedal-car that he used to drive up and down the Grand Corridor at Windsor Castle or around its gardens as the Queen looked laughingly on. But as he grew older, Windsor's state-rooms were to give the prince cause to reflect on the enormity of his future role. Anne, not burdened by the same concerns, was a more vivacious, boisterous and no-nonsense child, who took after her father. Charles's character was an echo of his mother's — gentle and even somewhat shy. Charles and Anne have, however, always been close.

Elizabeth and Philip chose to send Charles to school, making him the first heir apparent not educated by a private tutor. Anne was educated at home by a governess before attending Benenden School. The 1st Buckingham Palace Company of Brownies was re-formed so that Anne could socialise with girls her own age. Like her mother, Anne turned into an accomplished horsewoman, becoming the only member of the British royal family to compete in the Olympics. In addition, the Queen's only daughter carries out the most engagements and public appearances of any member of the royal family.

Meanwhile, Elizabeth's own devotion to duty means that her eldest son still awaits his royal destiny — indeed, in April 2011 he overtook his great-great-grandfather King Edward VII as the longest-serving heir apparent in British history.

Top left: The young family in 1951. Family time, generally restricted to the school holidays, was spent largely at Balmoral, and Sandringham, when both children learned to share their mother's love of countryside and outdoors pursuits.

Right: The new Queen with her young son and daughter in 1952. Charles was still blissfully unaware that his mother's accession had made him heir to the throne, as well as Duke of Cornwall and holder of five Scottish titles.

MOTHER
to Andrew and Edward

Left: A radiant Queen Elizabeth with four-year-old Prince Andrew and his newborn brother Edward in the Music Room of Buckingham Palace, where all four of her children were christened by the Archbishop of Canterbury. The Queen's sons were all born in the Palace, while Anne was born at nearby Clarence House.

Right: The Queen and Prince Philip with their youngest sons at the Queen's private residence Balmoral, where the royal family spend several weeks each summer. A peaceful retreat, the estate has scope for shooting, fishing, riding and other outdoor pursuits, as well as being the setting for countless family picnics over the years.

PRINCE ANDREW ARRIVED in 1960, 12 years after his brother Charles and four years before the Queen's last child, Edward. According to royal historian Robert Lacey, it was the Queen who insisted on "a second round" of children. In a handwritten letter to her second cousin Lady Mary Cambridge soon after Andrew's birth, Elizabeth told of how "the baby is adorable, and […] very good, and putting on weight well. Both the older children are riveted by him, and all in all, he's going to be terribly spoilt by all of us, I'm sure!"

Aged 38 and 12 years into her reign when Edward was born, the Queen was able to cut back on her royal duties and devote more time and attention to her younger sons than she had on Charles and Anne. She was also more confident as both mother and monarch by that time, and more adept at combining the two roles.

In spite of the age gap, the Queen's oldest and youngest sons Charles and Edward developed a close relationship, while Prince Andrew – often said to be the Queen's favourite son – was a childhood playmate of none other than Diana Spencer, who grew up practically next door to the Queen and her family, at Park House adjacent to Sandringham.

With the birth of Prince Andrew in 1960, the Queen became the first reigning sovereign to give birth to a child since Queen Victoria, whose youngest child, Princess Beatrice, was born in 1857.

With the birth of Prince Edward in 1964 the family was complete. The Queen wrote: "He is a great joy to us all, especially Andrew who is completely fascinated by him."

MOTHER-IN-LAW
A supportive role model

Elizabeth shares her LOVE OF HORSES *with two of her daughters-in-law. She* RIDES *with the Countess of Wessex and enjoys* EQUESTRIAN EVENTS *with the Duchess of Cornwall.*

A SUPREME GOVERNOR of the Church of England, the Queen has found the divorces of three of her four children challenging, but she has confronted the difficulties involved with her trademark equanimity and lightness of hand, and over the decades has shown genuine affection towards her children-in-law as well as providing them with inspiration and guidance.

The first of Elizabeth's children to marry was Anne, in 1973, to Mark Phillips, an aide-de-camp to the Queen. After the marriage broke down, Anne's second marriage in late 1992 brought some much-needed cheer to the royal family in the year that the Queen famously described as her 'annus horribilis' – the formal separation of Charles and Diana, after their unhappiness had become public knowledge, had been announced a few days before Anne's wedding. As Anne chose to marry Rear-Admiral Timothy Laurence (*above*) within the Church of Scotland, where remarriage of divorcees is less controversial, her mother and father were able to attend.

In becoming only the second senior British royal to re-marry after divorce (after Henry VIII four centuries before), Anne set the precedent for the second marriage of her older brother, to Camilla Parker Bowles in 2005. On the announcement of Charles's second marriage, the Queen offered her formal consent to the union, granted after consultation with the prime minister, and her congratulations. She and Philip were not able to attend the civil wedding ceremony but were present at the service of blessing and held a reception for the couple in Windsor Castle.

The Queen's relationships with her first daughters-in-law, Diana Spencer and Sarah Ferguson, were the most complex and highly charged, given the issues, controversies and personalities involved. But although she was very different to Diana temperamentally, the Queen was supportive of her both as a young bride coming to terms with her new life and duties, and during her marital difficulties. Similarly, she was very fond of Sarah Ferguson, who married Andrew in 1986, and though their relationship also had its ups and downs, Sarah earned the Queen's respect for remaining on good terms with her ex-husband as well as for her work as charity patron and spokesperson.

The Queen's ongoing warm relationship with the Countess of Wessex, wife to Edward since 1999, is a source of relief and comfort. The two women are known to share an interest in military history and horse-riding.

Top left: The Queen and the Princess of Wales stand outside Clarence House in August 1987, for the 87th birthday of the Queen Mother. The cracks in Princess Diana's marriage were not yet evident.

Top right: The Queen and the Duchess of York at Clarence House, 1986. When her son's divorce was announced in 1992, the Queen broke with normal protocol to express her personal unhappiness over the split.

Above left: The Queen and the Countess of Wessex wait to attend the Christmas Day service at Sandringham Church. The Countess rode in the State limousine with the Queen for this occasion.

Above right: The Queen with the Duchess of Cornwall, at Windsor Horse Show in 2011, when the Queen's horse St. James won two events. Both women are well known for their love of equestrianism.

GRANDMOTHER
A royal matriarch

"The Queen knows all her grandchildren use Facebook and it would be remiss of the Household not to be keeping up-to-date with the web."

A royal aide

Born first of the grandchildren, to Anne in 1977, Peter Phillips has always had a special place in the heart of both the Queen and Prince Philip, while Peter's sister Zara, five years his junior, followed in her grandmother's (and mother's) footsteps by becoming an accomplished horsewoman.

William, born in 1982, merits special attention given his likely future as King, but from christenings and graduations to airforce base visits, the Queen has always been there to support and advise both William and his brother Harry in their day-to-day lives. They, in turn, have helped the Queen get to grips with modern-day technology such as texting and tweeting. They defer to their grandmother's wisdom and authority, with Harry commenting in the run-up to his brother's wedding: "I will have a few stories. I think my grandmother will be there so I'll have to be selective."

In 1988 and 1990 came Beatrice and Eugenie, daughters to Andrew, the Queen's own reputed favourite. Close to both girls, Her Majesty until recently greatly enjoyed riding with them at Windsor Great Park – as she did with her youngest grandchildren, Edward and Sophie's daughter and son Louise and James, born in 2003 and 2007.

Top left: The Queen, with her grandchildren – Zara and Peter Phillips, Prince William and Prince Harry – at Sandringham for Christmas 1988.

Above: The Queen with Prince William and Prince Harry at the Trooping the Colour ceremony.

Right: The Queen poses for a horseback portrait with daughter Anne and granddaughter Zara Phillips at Windsor Castle to mark her 78th birthday in 2004. In a neat parallel, Her Majesty's 20-year-old mare Tinkerbell is mother to Anne's mount, Peter Pan, and to Zara's Tiger Lily.

STATE VISITS

The Queen has probably made more visits to other countries and experienced more state banquets, handshakes, entertainments, troop inspections, national anthems and the like than any other head of state. Her schedule of royal tours of Commonwealth countries and state visits to foreign nations began just after her ascent to the throne in 1952 and has continued to the present day. Nor have her trips been merely ornamental: behind many of them has lain serious diplomacy, from repairing the diplomatic damage caused by the Suez Crisis in 1956 to restoring political confidence and maintaining the momentum of the Peace Process on her state visit to the Republic of Ireland in 2011.

THE 1950s
To the Commonwealth and beyond

"If you have had a moment in your hectic schedules to read any of our newspapers, you know that you both have captivated the people of our country by your charm and graciousness."
President Dwight D. Eisenhower, 1957

IN NOVEMBER 1953 – only a few months after the nation had been putting up bunting and organising street parties for her coronation – Queen Elizabeth set out on the most ambitious tour of the Commonwealth ever taken. It lasted almost half a year, covered 43,618 miles and included visits to a dozen countries, from Bermuda and the Coco Islands to New Zealand and Australia.

The Queen and Prince Philip first flew to the Caribbean where, in Jamaica, they boarded HMS Gothic, their floating home for most of the trip. They sailed through the Panama Canal to Fiji and Tonga, where one of the exhibits on show was a giant turtle said to have been alive in the days of Captain Cook. The royal couple arrived in New Zealand on 23rd December, and the Queen made the traditional royal Christmas broadcast from Auckland. The couple spent four weeks in the land of the 'long white cloud' before enjoying a two-month stay in Australia, where an estimated three-quarters of the population greeted them with wild enthusiasm. The return journey included stops at Ceylon (Sri Lanka), Aden, Uganda, Malta and Gibraltar, from where they sailed to London on the new Royal Yacht *Britannia*, launched the previous year.

In 1955 the Queen was back on the royal road, this time to Norway, then in the following year she made a state visit to Nigeria, the largest of Britain's African colonies. The trip ended in the capital of Lagos with a spectacular dance of thousands of masked warriors.

Paris in the spring beckoned in 1957, where the Queen and the Duke met President René Coty. Highlights included a boat ride along the Seine, a banquet in Versailles and an inspection of a car factory and the Venus de Milo. The Queen was the first British monarch to visit France since Queen Victoria in 1855 and was greeted by rapturous crowds. She did much to rebuild Britain's friendship with France after the fiasco of the Suez Crisis the year before – as she did when she visited the USA in October 1957.

The Queen and Prince Philip returned to North America in June 1959, by which time the Queen was pregnant with her third child, the future Prince Andrew. The royal couple spent six weeks in Canada, visiting every province and territory, and made a fleeting visit to Chicago. The first seven years of her reign had taken her to all parts of the globe, and her charm had extended farther.

Top left: The Queen and the Duke of Edinburgh wave to crowds in Winnipeg on their visit to Canada in 1959. During their stay, the Queen and the US President Dwight D. Eisenhower opened the St. Lawrence Seaway – a system of locks, canals and channels giving access from the Atlantic to the Great Lakes – with a short cruise aboard *Britannia*.

Above left: Queen Elizabeth and Oba Adele, the sovereign of Lagos, greet the crowds during the start of the royal tour to Nigeria in 1956. The Queen was well prepared for the heat, with Norman Hartnell, her dressmaker, making a mobile stage-cum-canopy to give much-needed shade during the various tribal ceremonies she had to attend. Perhaps the most significant moment of the tour was a visit to a leper community, which did much to dispel popular fears of leprosy as a contagious disease.

Above right: The US Vice-President Richard Nixon leads the Queen up the steps of the Capitol in Washington for a reception in October 1957. The Queen and Prince Philip were visibly relaxed on their US visit, dropping in on shops and football games, and charming those they met. They joined the 350th anniversary celebrations at Jamestown, Virginia, and the Governor, Thomas B. Stanley, wrote: "No visitor to our shores has ever so quickly and completely captured all our hearts and claimed such willing admiration and respect."

THE 1960s
Strengthening ties, healing wounds

Left: The Queen and Prince Philip share a joke during their visit to West Africa in November 1961. At Freetown, Sierra Leone, a flotilla of small boats festooned with Union Jacks rowed out to welcome *Britannia*. The royal couple enjoyed displays of dancing and traditional stilt-walking as well as a trip to a diamond mine.

Right: The Queen addresses a gathering of more than a quarter of a million in Delhi on her visit to India in January and February 1961. During her stay the Queen planted a tree at the Gandhi Memorial and, with Prince Philip, gazed into a pool at the Taj Mahal, decades before Princess Diana was memorably photographed there.

THE 1960s – THE DECADE OF POP CULTURE, hippies, the Vietnam War and widespread student unrest – provided a less certain backdrop to the Queen's visits and tours. These were still made with impeccable orchestration and received with enthusiasm, whether in the Antipodes in 1963, the Caribbean in 1966 or Brazil and Chile in 1968, but notes of dissent crept in. The royal couple were criticised at home for participating in a tiger hunt in India in 1961, and in 1964 the Queen found herself being booed in Quebec City by Quebec separatists.

Nevertheless, the royal couple continued to charm and impress their hosts. The Duke played polo in Lahore during the visit to the Indian sub-continent, while the Queen gamely rode on an elephant. Later in 1961 they visited Ghana, Sierra Leone and the Gambia. There they acknowledged Britain's role in African history by inspecting the ruins of James Island – a former British fort and slave port.

But arguably the most successful visit in the 1960s was that to West Germany in 1965. In Berlin, huge crowds cheered the Queen and chanted "Elisabet, Elisabet". She planted a tree hoping that "this one will be symbolic of a new chapter of understanding and co-operation between our two countries."

In 1961 the Queen made the first ever visit to Ghana by a British sovereign. The political situation was volatile, and the British press were concerned that her visit might be seen to endorse the undemocratic and dictatorial regime.

The visit was a huge success; even the neo-Marxist *Ghana News* declared that the people of Ghana had been moved by this "most modest and lovable of sovereigns".

THE 1970s
Jubilee and discontent

Left: The Queen drinks a cup of tea in the Garden of the Katsura Imperial Villa in Kyoto during her visit to Japan in May 1975. This was not the traditional British 'cuppa' but a delicate green tea, given as part of the Japanese tea ceremony, a ritual influenced by Zen Buddhism.

In the 1970s alone the Queen made STATE VISITS *to a total of 24 countries, starting with* TURKEY *and ending with* ZAMBIA.

WITH ITS LITANY of miners' strikes, electricity cuts, the three-day working week, soaring oil prices and roaring inflation, the 1970s was one of the most turbulent decades of recent British history. Amid the doom and gloom, however, the Queen's Silver Jubilee in 1977 temporarily lit up the nation as celebrations took place throughout Britain and the Commonwealth. During that year, the Queen and Prince Philip travelled an estimated 56,000 miles, from the Antipodes to the Caribbean, and were greeted by cheering, flag-waving crowds everywhere. She made her last stop in Barbados, where, two years previously, she had knighted the great West Indian cricketer Gary Sobers at the crowded Garrison Savannah racecourse.

If 1977 was the most demanding – and rewarding – period for royal visits abroad, the other years of the decade also proved to be busy for the Queen and the Duke. In early 1972, for example, the royal couple and Princess Anne, then 21 years old, travelled to Singapore and Malaysia. In May of the same year the Queen, the Duke and Prince Charles visited France, which gave the Queen the chance to pay her respects to her terminally-ill uncle, the Duke of Windsor, who as Edward VIII had abdicated from the throne in 1936.

In February 1975 the Queen visited Mexico, where she absorbed some of the country's ancient Maya culture at the ruined city of Uxmal. Then in May she was off to Japan, paying her respects to Emperor Hirohito and visiting the cities of Tokyo, Osaka, Ise and Kyoto. In the following year she and Prince Philip crossed the Atlantic to join in the United States' bicentennial celebrations. Their packed six-day tour included a visit to Monticello, the home of Thomas Jefferson, principal author of the Declaration of Independence and a moving force behind wresting America away from the royal authority of the Queen's ancestor, King George III.

Arguably the most important state visit of the decade, however, came in February 1979, when the Queen travelled to the oil-producing nations of Kuwait, Bahrain, Saudi Arabia, Qatar, the United Arab Emirates and Oman. The price of oil had been a key factor in Britain's industrial turmoil during the decade and it was hoped that the royal tour would strengthen Anglo-Arab relationships. The Queen already knew a few of the Gulf States' rulers through the world of horse breeding and racing, and both she and the Duke seemed genuinely interested in the entertainments laid on for them, from sword dances to camel racing. To the relief of the UK government, the trip was a great success.

Above: Dressed in a traditional Maori cloak, a radiant Queen Elizabeth attends a ceremony in New Zealand in February 1977, the year of her Silver Jubilee. Her visit to the Antipodes drew huge crowds and revealed a human side not often seen in public. As Ronald Allison, the BBC's Court correspondent at the time, reported: "Suddenly the lady on the schoolroom wall, on the postage stamp, was a real person, who drove cars, barbecued, had a bit of a sense of humour."

Above: The Queen is given the red-carpet treatment in Saudi Arabia as she is greeted by King Khalid during her visit to the kingdom in February 1979. Her long dress reflects sensitivities to the Islamic culture of the country. The trip was made against a backdrop of the Iranian revolution in the previous month and did much to reassure the Gulf States of Britain's support for them. The Queen flew out to the Middle East on Concorde – a conscious decision to showcase the best of British technology – before joining up with the Royal Yacht *Britannia*.

THE 1980s
Breaking new ground

"I render homage to the Christian history of your people, as well as to their cultural achievements. The ideals of freedom and democracy, anchored in your past remain challenges for every generation of upright citizens in your land."
Pope John Paul II, 1980

Despite the formality and protocol of the royal tours in the 1980s, the world of royalty was merging with the world of celebrity. In California in 1983 more than 3,000 journalists from around the world gathered to report the royal visit, which included a trip to President Ronald Reagan's ranch and a banquet at which Frank Sinatra entertained the Queen.

Otherwise, the Queen's travels abroad continued to reflect the politics of the time. The autumn Commonwealth tour in 1982, for example, which included Australia and Papua New Guinea, was lightened by the euphoria in Britain after victory in the Falklands war in the spring. The same feel-good factor fed into the Queen's visit to the USA in February 1983, although the Anglo-America bonhomie was severely tested later on in the year, when US troops invaded the Commonwealth country of Grenada in the Caribbean.

Twice in the decade the Queen broke new ground. In 1980 she became the first British sovereign and head of the Church of England to make a state visit to the Vatican, where she had private talks with Pope John Paul II. Then in 1986 she became the first British monarch ever to visit China, bringing a rarely-seen royal glitter to the Land of the Dragon.

Above left: Pope John Paul II talks with Queen Elizabeth – in a long black gown to comply with Vatican dress codes – on 17 October 1980. The Queen gave the Pope a book about Windsor Castle; he presented a facsimile of the manuscript of Dante's *Divine Comedy*.

Above: The Queen makes her way by native canoe to Tuvalu, a group of South Pacific islands, in 1982. Tuvalu became an independent Commonwealth nation in 1978. The Queen's visit was made shortly after she had opened the Commonwealth Games in Brisbane, Australia.

Left: The Queen's visit to China in October 1986 came shortly after fractious negotiations about transferring the sovereignty of Hong Kong to China. Received in Beijing by President Li Xiannian, the Queen and Prince Philip did much to smooth relations between the two countries.

The Queen and Prince Philip were given an exclusive trip to the Great Wall and a tour of the Forbidden City in Beijing, the seat of the Chinese emperors from medieval times to the abdication of the last Chinese emperor, Puyi, in 1912. The Terracotta Army in Shaanxi province was one of the highlights of their visit. The Queen was given the rare privilege of being allowed to walk among the warriors. As the UK Foreign Secretary Sir Geoffrey Howe, who accompanied the royal party, remarked: "It was almost as if we were part of the army".

At the end of the state visit, the royal couple invited members of the Chinese government to a banquet on board the Royal Yacht *Britannia*, moored in Shanghai.

THE 1990s
Post-Cold War reconciliation

Left: The Queen and Prince Philip visiting the Khayelitsha Township, South Africa, in March 1995, just a year after South Africa had re-joined the Commonwealth. The six-day trip was the first to South Africa by a reigning British monarch in 48 years. About 1,000 people lined the township roads, with some climbing on walls and roofs to see the Queen. She visited a centre in Khayelitsha township where poor mothers learnt job skills. The women at the township's Philani feeding centre lined their hand-woven mats along the ground for the monarch and sang and danced as the Queen toured the premises.

THE 1990s SAW A GREAT DEAL of political turbulence in Europe after the end of the Cold War, and state visits by the Queen helped to forge better UK relations with some of the countries experiencing extraordinary change, including Russia and a reunified Germany. The Queen and Prince Philip visited the latter in 1992 and received a mixed reception.

Two years later, in 1994, the royal couple travelled to Russia to meet President Boris Yeltsin, who hoped the visit would be seen as an endorsement of his pro-democracy policies. The crowds on the streets were curious and friendly, and the two British royals tactfully avoided any reference to the Bolshevik murder of Czar Nicholas II and his family, to whom they were both distantly related. "You can't condemn a whole nation for what a few extremists do or did," the Prince told one UK reporter.

Another country that had emerged from political turbulence was the new post-apartheid South Africa, and the Queen was welcomed there in March 1995 by President Nelson Mandela. It was the first time she had visited since 1947, when she had celebrated her 21st birthday. Delighted township crowds waved banners saying "Thank you for coming back".

On a state visit to Germany in 1992 crowds waved Union Jacks and cheered in Berlin. But in Dresden – where a firestorm following Allied bombing in February 1945 killed some 25,000 people – some boos rang out, and an egg was thrown.

The Queen and Prince Philip attended a sevice in Dresden's Kreuzkirche to commemorate the bombing, conducted by both German and British clergy. Prince Philip gave a blessing in German, while the governor of the state of Saxony responded in English.

Above: The Queen, resplendent in fur, inspects a guard of honour at Vnukovo Airport, Moscow, at the start of her four-day state visit to Russia in October 1994. In a speech to schoolchildren, the Queen emphasised the historical links between Britain and Russia:

"The ambassadors and merchant venturers of Queen Elizabeth I first came to Russia 400 years ago. Europe was emerging from the long winter of the Middle Ages into an age of discovery and innovation. I should like to think that we stand on the threshold of another such age."

Above: Accompanied by the German President Richard von Weizsaecker, the Queen chats with schoolchildren in front of the Brandenburg Gate in Berlin during her state visit to Germany in October 1992. She later walked through the Gate into East Berlin and was greeted with shouts of "Welcome!" by members of a several-thousand-strong crowd. The Queen's visit came at a time of tension between the UK and German governments, particularly over a lack of agreement concerning the new European jet fighter project.

THE 21ST CENTURY
Towards the Diamond Jubilee

Left: During her state visit to Ireland in 2011, the Queen was shown around the National Stud in Co. Kildare, where she saw the stud's most prized sire, Invincible Spirit. Other highlights of her Irish stay were visits to the medieval ruins on the Rock of Cashel in Co. Tipperary and the bustling English Market in Cork City.

Below: Queen Elizabeth II walks away from a replica of the *Susan Constant*, one of the three English ships that made a landfall on what was later named Virginia on 4 May 1607. In May 2007 the Queen visited the state for the first time in 50 years to commemorate the 400th anniversary of the settlement of Jamestown.

I N THE FIFTH DECADE of her reign, the Queen – still fit and full of stamina despite her advancing years – kept up her demanding schedule of overseas visits. The highlight of the first half of the Noughties was the 2002 tour of Commonwealth realms, carried out as part of the Queen's Golden Jubilee celebrations. Later on in the decade, in 2007, the Queen and Prince Philip marked two 400th anniversaries. The first was that of the English Church in Amsterdam, founded in 1607 to serve the city's English-speaking population. The second was the settlement of Jamestown in Virginia, USA. In October of the same year the Queen made a historic trip to Slovenia and Slovakia, becoming the first British monarch to visit those countries.

The most groundbreaking visit of the decade occurred in May 2011, when the Queen and Prince Philip flew to the Republic of Ireland, the first visit by a British monarch since the country gained its independence in 1922. The trip was intended to promote Anglo-Irish friendship and support the Peace Process in Northern Ireland. It was a resounding success. The Queen paid her respects to Irish republican heroes in Dublin's Garden of Remembrance and even spoke a few words of Irish at a state banquet – prompting the Irish President Mary McAleese to utter "Wow" three times.

Left: Queen Elizabeth and President Ivan Gasparovic of Slovakia tour Hrebienok, a ski resort in the Tatara Mountains, on 24 October 2008. In the Slovak capital of Bratislava the Queen met veterans of the Second World War as well as Sir Nicholas Winton, the 'British Schindler' who helped more than 650 Jewish children escape from the Nazis to Britain from Czechoslovakia.

At a formal banquet in the evening, the Queen said: "Here on the River Danube, Slovaks have long been at the crossroads of history. You have witnessed the coronation of kings and queens, the signing of peace treaties, and – dare I say – invasion from every quarter. Caught behind a line dividing East from West for so long, Slovakia has now asserted its place in a common European home in less turbulent times."

THE PUBLIC FACE

Queen Elizabeth's life is lived in the public view and this is nowhere more apparent than in the relentless annual round of state banquets, charity galas, command performances and garden parties. Yet, despite the formality of these carefully orchestrated occasions, the Queen succeeds in making personal contact with everyone she meets, from the heads of state that attend the royal banquets and the prime ministers she has met weekly throughout her reign to the ordinary people who greet her on walkabouts, line up to meet her at charity galas, or enjoy her hospitality at Buckingham Palace.

STATE BANQUETS
Entertaining on a grand scale

Left: The Queen hosted a state banquet for US President Barack Obama, when he made a state visit to the UK in May 2011. A total of 171 guests were treated to a menu of sole in crayfish sauce, followed by new season Windsor lamb with basil, sautéed courgettes and radishes, green beans, potatoes and salad. There was a vanilla and cherry charlotte dessert and wine from Ridgeview, a Sussex vineyard.

Below: The President of Ghana, John Agyekum Kufuor, with the Queen at a state banquet at Buckingham Palace in 2007. The 'white tie and decorations' dress code embraces national dress.

Right: The state banquet held at Windsor for President Nicolas Sarkozy on 26 March 2008 was the 97th hosted by the Queen since her accession in 1952.

ORE THAN 50,000 visitors a year pass through Buckingham Palace as guests at banquets, lunches, dinners, receptions and garden parties. The Queen hosts state banquets on the first day of state visits. These take place in the Ballroom at Buckingham Palace, which opened in 1856 with a ball to celebrate the end of the Crimean War, or at Windsor Castle.

Around 170 guests are invited to state banquets, which follow a formula that dates to the reign of Queen Victoria. Guests are first received by the Queen and the visiting head of state in the Palace's Music Room, before joining a procession, led by the Lord Chamberlain and Lord Steward, to the Ballroom. Before the meal commences, the Queen proposes a toast to her guest, who reciprocates. Throughout the meal there is a musical accompaniment, provided by a military orchestra in the gallery, and at the end of the meal, pipers process around the room. The guests then move to the State Dining Room and the Blue Drawing Room for coffee.

The planning for a state banquet begins six months before the event. Preparations include polishing 1,000 glasses, folding around 170 napkins and creating 20 flower displays. The Queen takes a close interest in all aspects of planning.

PRIME MINISTER MEETINGS
Working at the heart of Government

Left: Prime Minister David Cameron with the Queen at a visit to 10 Downing Street, on 21 June 2011. Photographs of past prime ministers adorn the staircase – the Queen has liaised with twelve prime ministers over her long reign.

As a BRITISH PASSPORT *is issued in the name of* HER MAJESTY, *it is unnecessary for the Queen to possess one. All other members of the* ROYAL FAMILY *have passports.*

LTHOUGH THE QUEEN is a constitutional monarch, and therefore polically neutral, she nevertheless gives a weekly audience to the prime minister, at which she has a right and a duty to express her views on Government matters. She also plays a role in the mechanics of calling a general election when the prime minister must request the sovereign to grant a dissolution of Parliament. After the election the appointment of the prime minister is also the prerogative of the sovereign – constitutional conventions dictate that this is a person who commands the confidence of the House of Commons, normally the leader of the party with an overall majority. After the appointment is accepted, the Court Circular reports that "the Prime Minister Kissed Hands on Appointment".

Over the course of her reign, the Queen has had relationships with twelve British prime ministers: Winston Churchill 1951–55; Sir Anthony Eden 1955–57; Harold Macmillan 1957–63; Sir Alec Douglas-Home 1963–64; Harold Wilson 1964–70 and 1974–76; Edward Heath 1970–74; James Callaghan 1976–79; Margaret Thatcher 1979–90; John Major 1990–97; Tony Blair 1997–2007; Gordon Brown 2007–2010; David Cameron from 2010. Details of the meetings are strictly confidential, but successive prime ministers have been impressed by the Queen's diligence and grasp of detail. She is an assiduous reader of official briefs, and is always well-informed and accessible.

The Queen's first prime minister, Winston Churchill, was undoubtedly one of her favourites. He became a father figure to the new Queen, but was also deferential and courteous. He visited her in Balmoral during the first year of her reign, where he got to know her well. For the Queen, Churchill was a monumental British figure, a towering wartime leader and defender of the British Empire. She was captivated by his erudition, grasp of history and sense of humour; they also shared a passion for horse-racing.

More surprisingly, the Queen also formed a close friendship with the Labour leader, Harold Wilson. Despite the fact that they had very little in common, the two shared a rapport. Wilson was warm-hearted, witty and communicative, and helped to make her feel in touch with her people. Audiences that normally lasted 30 minutes extended to two hours. Harold Wilson commented: "You realise very quickly that she is a unique repository of knowledge… and what emerges is a combination of experience, very hard work, a good memory and good judgement – both about things and about people."

Above: Prime Minister Margaret Thatcher is joined by the Queen and five former PMs at 10 Downing Street, London, as she hosts a dinner celebrating the 250th anniversary of the residence becoming the London home of prime ministers. Margaret Thatcher was the Queen's first female prime minister; however, they were very different. Thatcher was a missionary and an iconoclast, while the Queen is conservative and wary of change.

Left: Queen Elizabeth, with Prince Charles and Princess Anne, talks to Sir Winston Churchill in 1953, shortly after her accession to the throne. In February 1952, in an Address of Sympathy on her father's death, he commented: "A fair and youthful figure, Princess, wife and mother, is heir to all our traditions and glories never greater than in her father's days, and to all our perplexities and dangers never greater in peacetime than now."

WALKABOUTS
Meeting the people

Left: Queen Elizabeth II visits RAF Marham on 30 January 2002, on the first public engagement of her Golden Jubilee year. During the course of the year she took part in 50 walkabouts, met with people of all ages, religions and nationalities, travelled on myriad modes of transport, hosted numerous receptions, garden parties and two major concerts.

Right: Queen Elizabeth II, smiling while holding a small bouquet of flowers, on her arrival in Port Moresby, Papua New Guinea, 13 October 1982. Her Majesty is known in the pidgin language of Tok Pisin as 'Missis Kwin', and as 'Mama belong big family'.

PLUNGING UNEXPECTEDLY into a crowd of Great War veterans, King George VI and Queen Elizabeth were the first royals to engage in a 'walkabout' in May 1939 on a visit to Ottawa, in Canada. As they shook hands and chatted with thrilled old soldiers, they had set a precedent, but it was over 30 years before the practice of moving through crowds and engaging spontaneously with ordinary people became the royal norm.

The first planned 'royal walkabout' took place during the visit by the Queen and the Duke of Edinburgh to Australia and New Zealand in 1970. The practice was introduced to allow them to meet a greater number of people, not simply officials and dignitaries.

Members of the public love royal walkabouts because they appear to be impromptu, a departure from the carefully scripted and choreographed itinerary. They are able to exchange words with the Queen, hand her bouquets and presents, have their photographs taken. Security personnel and ladies-in-waiting follow closely in the Queen's footsteps, ready to step in if danger threatens, or at the very least take charge of the growing armfuls of flowers and gifts that are presented to her.

The Queen has no opportunity to mix, unrecognised, amongst ordinary people. But, on 8 May 1945, she and her sister Margaret staged a truly impromptu 'walkabout', when they slipped out of the Palace and joined the jubilant VE-Day throngs.

They were accompanied by Corporal Wilds, Churchill's dispatch rider, who later reported that the princesses had been out on the streets, unrecognised, for two hours: "…the two princesses were missing. And no one knew where they were…"

CHARITY PATRON
A lifetime of service

MEMBERS OF THE ROYAL FAMILY have lent their names to organisations through formal patronages since the 18th century. The first recorded patronage was George II's involvement with the Society of Antiquaries, an organisation concerned with architectural and art history and conservation.

Royal involvement with other organisations has a long historical precedent: William IV became patron of The Royal United Services Institute for Defence and Security Studies; Queen Victoria became patron of the Mothers' Union in 1898. The Queen is patron of both these organisations today.

The Queen alone is patron of over 600 charities; the royal family between them lend their support to some 3,000. Patronages of many of the Queen's charities were inherited from George VI on Elizabeth's accession to the throne. Her patronage has been lent to a wide range of organisations, from hospitals, including the Queen Elizabeth Hospital for Children, to animal charities, including the RSPCA, Battersea Dogs Home and the Kennel Club, to campaigning charities, such as the Campaign to Protect Rural England. She is also the patron of many educational institutions, including the aptly named Queens' College in Cambridge.

On her Golden Jubilee, the Queen asked that people wishing to commemorate the occasion made a contribution to five of her favourite charities: Barnardo's, CRUSE Bereavement Services, I CAN (helping children with speech and language difficulties), the Royal Agricultural Benevolent Institution, and the Soldier, Sailors, Airmen and Families Association.

In 2002 the Queen even took the unusual step of writing a foreword to the "tempting array of recipes" in an Indian cookery book, published in support of another charity for which she is patron, Cancer Research UK. She is said to be a fan of Indian food.

A royal charity patron, in particular the Queen, will help immeasurably with attracting funds, as well as keeping volunteers – the bedrock of any charity – happy. Royal patrons are no longer passive figureheads; since the 1980s they have become much more involved in the business of running the charity, and have taken a very active part in fund-raising and public awareness drives. When the Queen is invited to preside at a charity gala, fund-raising dinner, prize-giving or grand opening, the public will flock in, there will be coverage in the media, and donations will multiply. The impact of the Queen's patronage is incalculable.

Far left: The Queen, patron of the Royal College of Music, watches her mother receive an honorary degree in 1973. The Royal College of Music was founded in 1882 under the patronage of the Prince of Wales.

Left: The Queen meets staff at the Royal Marsden Hospital in Chelsea, London. The Queen is the patron of the pioneering cancer rehabilitation centre which was founded by Dr. William Marsden in 1851 and granted its Royal Charter of Incorporation by King George V in 1910.

Left: The Queen visits the Royal Horticultural Society Garden at Wisley, Surrey accompanied by the Society's President, Peter Buckley. As RHS Patron, she officially opened The Glasshouse in celebration of the garden's bicentennial year on 26 June 2007. The history of the RHS dates to 1804, when the Horticultural Society of London was founded by Sir Joseph Banks and John Wedgwood. Its aim was to collect plant information and encourage the improvement of horticultural practice. After a period of financial crisis Prince Albert, its then President, revived its fortunes by arranging a new charter in 1861, resulting in the name, the Royal Horticultural Society.

CHARITY GALAS
Royal entertainment on command

Left: Queen Elizabeth meets the Blue Man Group and other performers backstage after the Royal Variety Performance in Cardiff in 2005. The Royal Variety Performance takes place in a different UK theatre each year. In 1955 there were two performances: one in London and one in Blackpool, the first time the event had ever been staged outside the capital.

Right: Queen Elizabeth with Sir Laurence Olivier in 1955. She was attending the world premiere of his film *Richard III,* in aid of King George's pension fund for actors and actresses. Members of the royal family often visit film premieres as a way of lending their support to the charity with which they are connected.

ROYAL COMMAND PERFORMANCES are the highlight of many performers' year, the chance to showcase their talents in front of a royal audience, with all the media coverage and positive publicity that inevitably follows.

Queen Elizabeth has been attending the Royal Variety Performance since her childhood (she now alternates with the Prince of Wales) and the proceeds of the performance are donated to the Entertainment Artistes' Benevolent Fund, which cares for hundreds of entertainers throughout the UK who need help and assistance as a result of old age, ill-health, or hard times. She has witnessed performances from an extraordinary range of performers, from Gracie Fields, Arthur Askey and Morecambe & Wise to Bette Midler, Whoopi Goldberg and Lady Gaga.

The Royal Film performance dates back to 1896 when the Prince of Wales and 40 royal guests watched a number of short films. The current run of Royal Film Performances in aid of the CTBF (Cinematograph Television Benevolent Fund) began in 1946 when King George VI, as Patron, and Queen Elizabeth took their daughters to see David Niven and Marius Goring in *A Matter of Life and Death.*

The Royal Variety Performance originated in 1912, when King George V attended a 'Royal Command Performance' at the Palace Theatre in Cambridge Circus.

It flourished under royal patronage throughout the 1920s and '30s, but the outbreak of war led to its cancellation from 1939–1945. In 1952 the first Variety Performance of the Queen's reign featured Norman Wisdom, the Beverley Sisters and Tony Hancock. The Queen pronounced it "the best show of all".

LAUNCHES AND OPENINGS
Ceremonial celebrations

The Queen has LAUNCHED 24 SHIPS *in her lifetime. The* FIRST SHIP *which she named as Queen was Her Majesty's Yacht* BRITANNIA, *which was launched from Clydebank in 1953.*

SHIP LAUNCHES, with their attendant brass bands, champagne bottles and festive celebrations, are very much part of the Queen's history. She watched, in 1938, as her mother launched the original Cunard liner *Queen Elizabeth*. The microphone her mother was using broke down, so the crowd did not hear her announcement, which was drowned out by the sound of the huge ship thundering down the slipway.

Princess Elizabeth launched her first ship, *HMS Vanguard*, in November 1944, aged just 18. She went on to launch four Cunard ocean liners: *Caronia* in 1947 (her last public engagement before her marriage); *Queen Elizabeth 2* in 1967; *Queen Mary 2* in 2004 and *Queen Elizabeth* in 2010.

Legend has it that the original intention in 1967 was simply to name the new liner *Queen Elizabeth*. The name was handed to the Queen in a sealed envelope, and it was traditional to add the name to the ship's bow after the ceremony. The Queen did not read the contents of the envelope and announced "I name this ship Queen Elizabeth the Second. May God bless her and all who sail in her." So the ship was effectively christened *Queen Elizabeth 2* (QE2) and became the most famous Cunard liner.

Over her long reign the Queen has added royal lustre to a great number of ribbon-cutting and unveiling ceremonies. As with ship launchings, these occasions provide a highly photogenic moment and add the royal imprimatur and seal of approval to public achievements, artistic endeavours, new constructions and new inventions.

In 2009 there was a much more personal moment when the Queen unveiled a statue of the Queen Mother, by the sculptor Philip Jackson, which stands just off The Mall in central London, next to a statue of her father King George VI. This was a historic moment as it was the first statue of a royal consort in London for over a century. The national memorial was funded by the sale of a special £5 coin to commemorate the Queen's 80th birthday in 2007.

Top left: In 1994 the Queen and President Mitterand of France cut the ribbon to officially open the Channel Tunnel. The Queen travelled from the first Eurostar terminal in London's Waterloo station to Calais. Her train arrived at the same time as a train carrying President Mitterand from Paris. The two locomotives met nose to nose, and the two heads of state then cut red, white and blue ribbons to the accompaniment of their respective national anthems.

Above: On 7 March 1969 Queen Elizabeth opened London Underground's new Victoria line. She arrived with her entourage at Green Park station, put a coin in the ticket machine, descended by escalator to the station platform and boarded a brand new train for the journey to the newly built station at Oxford Circus. She travelled in the driver's cab. After making the return journey, Queen Elizabeth became the first reigning monarch to travel on the London Underground.

She had first travelled on the tube in May 1939, when she boarded an underground train accompanied by her governess Marion Crawford and her sister Princess Margaret.

Above: In 1960 the Queen launched Britain's first nuclear-powered submarine *HMS Dreadnought* at the Vickers-Armstrong yard at Barrow-in-Furness. The launch took place on Trafalgar Day, the 155th anniversary of the Battle of Trafalgar in which Admiral Nelson was killed. Huge crowds turned out to see the Queen, despite heavy rain, and gave her three cheers as the submarine was set afloat.

SPEECHES
Public discourse

"1992 is not a year on which I shall look back with undiluted pleasure. In the words of one of my more sympathetic correspondents, it has turned out to be an 'Annus Horribilis'. I suspect that I am not alone in thinking it so."
Queen Elizabeth II

INEVITABLY, THE QUEEN is called upon to make a great many public speeches. She is not a natural public speaker, and is always most comfortable reading speeches from notes. Most of her speeches are prepared by private secretaries, and she then reviews the draft and consults with the Duke of Edinburgh about alterations and amendments. In general, her tendency is to downplay florid language – she is a very honest woman who does not want to convey sentiments she does not feel.

Her downbeat approach to public speaking comes into its own when she makes her annual speech at the State Opening of Parliament. Bespectacled, and reading without emotion from notes, she manages to convey complete neutrality about the upcoming programme of legislation, as befits a constitutional monarch.

The Queen's Christmas broadcasts are the one occasion when she speaks more clearly with her own voice. They usually have a strong Christian framework, and draw on her own experiences and concerns. Her loyalty to her own armed forces and the Commonwealth, as well as her concern for the environment, are frequent themes that she explores in these seasonal broadcasts.

Nevertheless, some of the Queen's speeches have marked major milestones. Her 21st birthday speech, in April 1947, was delivered on tour in South Africa, and was a genuinely heartfelt avowal of her loyalty and commitment to her people and to the Commonwealth: "I can make my solemn act of dedication with a whole Empire listening. I should like to make that dedication now."

When Princess Diana died in a car crash, the public felt the royal family were not displaying appropriate emotion. The Queen made a moving speech on the occasion which turned the tide of opinion: "In good times and bad, she never lost her capacity to smile and laugh, nor to inspire others with her warmth and kindness."

Above: In May 1965 the Queen gives the inaugural speech at the Kennedy Memorial in Runnymede, Surrey, while the President's widow, Jackie Kennedy, looks on: "His abiding affection for Britain engendered an equal response on this side of the Atlantic."

Right: In 1992 the Queen delivers a speech after a Guildhall luncheon to mark the 40th anniversary of her accession to the throne. In the speech she coined the phrase 'Annus Horribilis' to describe a year blighted by family divorce and the Windsor Castle fire.

GARDEN PARTIES
Al fresco entertaining

Left: The Queen and Duke of Edinburgh walk past a croquet game and some artificial pink flamingoes — all props for the Children's Garden Party, held at Buckingham Palace, in 2006. The party featured a host of characters from children's books. The party was attended by 2,000 children and 1,000 adults, who were chosen through a national ballot.

EVERY YEAR QUEEN ELIZABETH and the Duke of Edinburgh invite over 30,000 people to Buckingham Palace and Holyrood House in a series of four garden parties. The tradition of holding royal garden parties at Buckingham Palace dates back to the 1860s. The invitees are individuals who are deemed to be making a special contribution to the people and communities of the United Kingdom, and represent a cross-section of British society. In some years, for example on the occasion of the 50th anniversary of the National Health Service, additional garden parties are held.

Invitations to royal garden parties are sent out by the Lord Chamberlain, and all the arrangements are planned by the Lord Chamberlain's Office. Gentlemen wear morning dress, lounge suits or uniform; ladies wear afternoon dress (usually with hats). National dress can also be worn.

After the playing of the National Anthem, the Queen and the Duke of Edinburgh circulate amongst their guests, each taking a different route. Random presentations are made so that everyone has an equal chance of speaking to Her Majesty and members of her family. Further guests are invited to join their hosts in the Royal Tea Tent.

Approximately 8,000 guests attend each royal garden party, which takes place between 4pm and 6pm. At a typical garden party, around 27,000 cups of tea, 20,000 sandwiches and 20,000 slices of cake are consumed. Some 400 waiting staff are involved in the serving. One of two military bands plays selections of music during the afternoon.

Buckingham Palace's garden covers 40 acres. It is home to 30 different species of bird and more than 350 different wild flowers.

Left: Queen Elizabeth attends her garden party at Buckingham Palace on 11 July 2006. On this occasion she was joined by Prince Charles and the Duchess of Cornwall – other members of the royal family frequently attend garden parties and greet members of the public.

Below left: Garden parties are also held in honour of the Queen on her state visits abroad. Wearing a hat designed by Frederick Fox, she attends a garden party at Eden Hall, the residence of the British High Commissioner, during a state visit to Singapore, 11 October 1989. The house once belonged to an expatriate rubber broker, named Vivian Bath. He decided to retire to Australia after the Second World War and sold Eden Hall to the British Government in 1957 for a nominal sum, with the stipulation that a plaque be installed at the bottom of the flagpole, which reads "May the Union Jack fly here forever".

HOME AND AWAY

From her earliest childhood the Queen has lived in an array of palaces, castles and mansions. Like much else in her life her homes are highly symbolic. In their lavish splendour they reflect the prestige and power of the monarchy and its historic significance. Balmoral and Sandringham, despite their grandeur, are private houses and royal retreats; with their hunting, shooting and fishing and scenic grounds they represent the rural idyll that successive generations of the monarchy have sought and treasured. Even when the Queen is on the move, she travels with a sense of majesty, as the Royal Yacht Britannia *and Royal Train attest.*

BUCKINGHAM PALACE
Ceremonial splendour

Left: A family gathering at Buckingham Palace in May 1942. The Queen is standing at the fireplace. As the Palace was a target of German bombs, valuables were removed or protected during the war years. The horses and carriages from the Royal Mews were moved to Windsor, where the horses were put to work on the farm. There was an air raid shelter at Buckingham Palace.

There are 1,514 DOORS and 760 WINDOWS in Buckingham Palace. All windows are cleaned EVERY SIX WEEKS. There are over 40,000 LIGHT BULBS in the Palace.

ONE OF THE FEW WORKING PALACES in the world today, Buckingham Palace is the Queen's London home as well as the working heart of the constitutional monarchy. Much of the ceremonial life of the monarchy is conducted here, from state banquets and investitures to garden parties and receptions.

When Elizabeth moved to Buckingham Palace as a girl, it was a daunting, monumental place, characterised by long, ill-lit corridors, gloomy barred windows and antiquated plumbing. Her parents soon set about decorating and modernising their living quarters and turning the vast monument into a home. Elizabeth and Margaret, meanwhile, delighted in racing down the long corridors, and exploring the magnificent 40-acre grounds, which included a large lake.

German bombers targeted the Palace, the symbolic heart of the monarchy, during the war and it suffered nine direct hits. King George VI's insistence on remaining in his London home, despite the danger, was greatly admired by the British public. When her father died, the Queen was expected to move from Clarence House to Buckingham Palace, despite Prince Philip's resistance. It had always been the monarch's home and represented continuity.

The principal suite of state rooms, at the rear of the Palace, centres on the bow-windowed Music Room, flanked by the Blue and White Drawing Rooms. The Picture Gallery, adorned by exhibits from the Queen's outstanding private collection, including works by Rembrandt, Van Dyck, Rubens, Canaletto and Vermeer, lies at the centre of the suite. Other rooms include the Green Drawing Room, the State Dining Room and the Throne Room. The 120ft-long Ballroom was opened by Queen Victoria in 1856 with a ball celebrating the end of the Crimean War. It is used for state banquets and formal receptions. Underneath the state rooms is a less grand suite of rooms, used for informal entertaining, while the Queen's private apartments are in the North Wing.

In all, the Palace contains 19 state rooms, 52 principal bedrooms, 188 staff bedrooms, 92 offices, and 78 bathrooms. It is the headquarters of the royal household, and the workplace of some 800 people. Every year, over 50,000 people visit the Palace as guests to banquets, lunches, dinners, receptions and the royal garden parties. In addition, the state rooms are open to the public in the summer. The balcony is world-famous, a venue for royal appearances since 1851, while the Palace remains a focal point for public gatherings at times of national celebration and tragedy.

Left: Princess Elizabeth working at her desk in Buckingham Palace, 19 July 1946. At the age of 19 she was given her own suite of rooms and two ladies-in-waiting, and embarked on a full diary of public engagements. She was allowed to choose the decor of her new rooms, but deferred to her mother's judgement. As a result they reflected her mother's taste: painted in pink and grey, with flowered chintzes.

Above: President Obama and Michelle Obama attend a state banquet hosted by the Queen in the Ballroom at Buckingham Palace on 24 May 2011. The 170 guests atttending the white tie dinner sat around tables arranged in a giant U-shape, with six crystal glasses per person and gold-plated cutlery. They were serenaded by an eclectic mixture of music played by the Band of the Scots Guards.

WINDSOR CASTLE
Medieval romance

"The most romantique castle that is in the world…"
Samuel Pepys, 1666

THE LARGEST OCCUPIED CASTLE in the world, Windsor Castle is an official residence of the Queen. She usually spends the weekends at Windsor, and every year takes up official residence there for a month over the Easter holiday, and also for a week in June when she presides over the Order of the Garter ceremony.

Windsor Castle has a special place in the Queen's heart. It is steeped in romance and history, tracing its origins back to William the Conqueror, who built a wooden castle keep on a chalk bluff rising above the River Thames. Its great bulk dominates the skyline, an accretion of medieval walls, towers and rooftops. Successive sovereigns have made their mark on the Castle. Edward III lavished vast sums of money on the Castle buildings, while Edward IV founded St. George's Chapel, the symbolic headquarters of the Knights of the Garter, in 1475. Charles II, asserting the restoration of the monarchy, made extensive alterations to the state apartments, creating a set of extravagant, baroque interiors. George III and George IV renovated and rebuilt Charles II's state apartments at colossal expense, producing the current design, a fine example of late Georgian taste, and an expression of the power and dominance of a nation that had emerged victorious from the recent Napoleonic Wars.

The Castle covers 13 acres and contains over 1,000 rooms. It is a kind of village, an eclectic jumble of buildings that span ten centuries of history. The lower ward includes the Albert Memorial Chapel and St. George's Chapel, the burial place of ten sovereigns. The upper ward includes the monarch's private apartments, visitors' apartments, and the royal library (home to the drawings, prints, manuscripts and books in the Royal Collection). The Castle is the headquarters of several departments of the royal household, and also houses the Royal Archives and Royal Photograph Collection. Over 350 people live there, from domestic staff and archivists to retired courtiers occupying grace-and-favour houses.

The Queen spent the war years at Windsor, along with her sister Margaret, and enjoyed riding in Windsor Great Park (*right*), putting on Christmas pantomimes and socialising with the Castle Company of the Grenadier Guards, whose job it was to guard the royal family. Today, she retreats to her beloved Castle for peaceful weekends, and on occasion hosts state visits for overseas monarchs or heads of state there, presiding over state banquets in St. George's Hall. The 1992 fire that caused damage to much of the upper ward was a devastating personal blow. Restoration works, paid for by opening Buckingham Palace to the public, cost £37 million.

SANDRINGHAM
A country retreat

"Because it's an inherited place, one's known it since one was a child. I know how much my father loved it…we are very involved with the people on the estate – you have a responsibility towards them."
Queen Elizabeth

A FAMILY HOME since the mid-19th century, Sandringham in Norfolk is a much-treasured rural retreat. Queen Victoria bought the property for her son the Prince of Wales in 1862. He felt the house was too small to accommodate his growing family, so he had the old house razed and commissioned the architect A.J. Humbert to design a new house. The result is a rambling neo-Jacobean mansion, built in red brick, with mock Elizabethan chimneys. Sandringham bears the imprint of successive generations of the royal family, from the Edwardian rococo of the drawing room to the pea-green dining room, hung with Goya tapestries, that is the legacy of the Queen Mother.

At 20,000 acres, Sandringham is one of the largest estates in Norfolk. There is excellent shooting, and venison from the estate is regularly sent to Buckingham Palace. The estate is also famous for its huge harvest of samphire and hazelnuts. Elizabeth is in charge of the horses, gun-dogs, cattle and pigs and also breeds and races racing pigeons there. Sandringham Church, just a few hundred yards from the house, is a monument to the people who have lived and worked on the estate, not least generations of royals, including both her grandfather and father, who died at Sandringham.

Top left: Elizabeth, with a faithful corgi, stands in front of Sandringham in 1982. She always spends the anniversary of her father's death, 6 February, at Sandringham.

Above: The Big Game Museum at Sandringham displays over 300 animals, many shot by members of the royal family. King Edward VII ordered the clocks at Sandringham to be set half an hour ahead of Greenwich Mean Time to allow more daylight for shooting.

Right: The Queen and Prince Philip at Sandringham in 1992, with Brandy the dorgi.

BALMORAL
A Scottish fantasy

Princess Elizabeth INVITED *Prince Philip to spend* THREE WEEKS *at Balmoral in the summer of 1946 for the* GROUSE-SHOOTING. *It was probably during this holiday that* HE PROPOSED.

SCOTLAND HAD A ROMANTIC ALLURE for Queen Victoria, who – with Prince Albert – bought the Balmoral estate on the banks of the River Dee in 1852. The old castle of Balmoral was demolished, and in its place a new castle was built in 1856. In Scots Baronial style, it is an elaborate, turreted, medieval fantasy – a fitting retreat for a Queen who had fallen in love with the Highlands and, following her husband's early death, was all too keen to escape from public expectations and duties.

Since then the Castle has been passed down by family inheritance; like Sandringham, Balmoral is one of the Queen's private family estates, and is not part of the Crown estate. Traditionally she spends the shooting season – August, September and part of October – in Scotland. The Castle is surrounded by a working estate of nearly 50,000 acres, managed by an official known as the Resident Factor. The estate includes Ballochbuie Forest, saved from timber cutters by Queen Victoria, the Loch Muick and Lochnagar Wildlife Reserve, and land maintained for deer, grouse and salmon. A malt whisky distillery located on the Balmoral Estate produces the Royal Lochnagar Single Malt whisky. More than 20 Highland, Fell and Haflinger ponies are kept for trekking and deer retrieval during the stalking season.

Queen Victoria's presence is very palpable at Balmoral; her specially designed thistle wallpaper still hangs on the wall, her tartan rugs and curtains are still in use, and her specially designed tartan and thistle chintzes still dominate the furnishings. Scottish landscape portraits adorn the wall, alongside endless ranks of antlers, and a statue of the Queen's great-great-grandmother and her consort still stands in the gardens. Queen Victoria created the Riverside Walk upriver from the Castle, along with a series of graceful suspension bridges, and it is still possible to walk in her footsteps.

The Queen has been visiting Balmoral every summer since her childhood, originally staying at Birkhall, a house on the Balmoral estate that is currently used by Prince Charles. The young Princess Elizabeth loved the outdoors life, the picnics on the shores of Loch Muick, the Scottish tea-time treats (scones, baps, bannocks), the venison for dinner and the pipe music that invariably accompanied the evening meal, played by the King's own tartan-clad pipers.

Today Balmoral is not just a holiday home for the royal family – providing shooting, beautiful scenery and the outdoors life that the Queen loves. It is also a well-managed working estate that attracts some 85,000 visitors a year.

Top left: The Queen and Prince Philip in the library of Balmoral Castle in 1977. Prince Philip is responsible to Elizabeth for the management of the estate, although she takes a keen personal interest in her highland cattle (she is patron of the Highland Cattle Society), ponies and Austrian Halflingers (which have chestnut coats and blond manes and tails).

Left: The Queen is pictured in 1967, in her characteristic Balmoral outfit – headscarf, kilt and wellington boots – at the North of Scotland Gun Dog Association Open Stake Retriever Trials in the grounds of Balmoral Castle. The Queen brings her labradors and spaniels with her to Balmoral, though they are said to howl plaintively at the sound of bagpipes.

Above: Seated comfortably on a tartan rug, members of the royal family play with Prince Andrew in the grounds of Balmoral. Picnicking has always played an important part in the life of Balmoral and barbecues are very popular. Prince Philip in particular loves outdoor cooking and has had a specially designed cast-iron barbecue made by the local blacksmith.

THE ROYAL YACHT
Life on the ocean wave

ONCE DESCRIBED AS A 'country house at sea', the Royal Yacht *Britannia* was a floating home for the Queen and her family for 44 years. The Queen was known to have great affection for a vessel that took her on nearly 700 trips abroad, from South Africa to Russia, and New Zealand to Canada, clocking up more than one million nautical miles along the way. When she launched it in April 1953 she said that "a yacht was a necessity, and not a luxury for the head of our great British Commonwealth, between whose countries the sea is no barrier, but the natural highway." By the mid-1990s, however, the high cost of running the ship became a matter of political debate, and in December 1997 *Britannia* was decommissioned at Portsmouth. A national competition was then held to find a permanent new home for the yacht and Edinburgh triumphed. The vessel is now moored in the city's port of Leith and serves as a major tourist attraction.

The tradition of royal yachts goes back to the days of Charles II, and there have been more than 80 vessels used by British sovereigns. *Britannia* was built by the Clyde shipbuilders John Brown & Co. at a cost of £2,098,000 and replaced the ageing *Victoria and Albert III*. The word 'yacht' may give the impression of a pleasure vessel, but *Britannia* served as a working palace, with enough room to hold substantial receptions, banquets and accommodate up to 250 guests. The Queen's designer Sir Hugh Casson created a mixture of style and comfort in the ship's interior, and its furniture included such choice items as Queen Victoria's satinwood desk and Hepplewhite chairs taken from *Victoria and Albert III*. A staff of up to 45 members of the royal household made the royal family and their guests comfortable, while a crew of about 240 Royal Yachtsmen went about their work as quietly as possible, wearing soft-soled plimsolls and giving hand signals rather than shouting orders.

Britannia did not function solely for royal tours and ambassadorial duties. It also provided glamorous honeymoon accommodation for four royal couples, Princess Margaret and Antony Armstrong-Jones (1960), Princess Anne and Captain Mark Phillips (1973), the Prince and Princess of Wales (1981), and the Duke and Duchess of York (1986). Nor did the royal tradition of nautical romance end with *Britannia*'s decommissioning: in July 2011 Zara Phillips, the daughter of Princess Anne, and her fiancé Mike Tindall hosted a cocktail party for 150 guests on the yacht in Edinburgh, adding another glitzy chapter to the Royal Yacht *Britannia*'s distinguished history at the heart of the royal family.

Left: The Queen boards *Britannia* in August 1995. Royal Yachtsmen had a distinctive uniform, which included a black silk bow tied at the back – an item originally worn as a token of mourning for the death of Prince Albert.

Right: *Britannia* leaves Portsmouth for the Western Isles of Scotland in August 1997. The Queen loved her annual cruises around the islands and shed public tears when *Britannia* was decommissioned a few months later.

Below: *Britannia*'s cosy rooms, including the state room shown here, displayed gifts from around the world, family photographs, various heirlooms and even a baby grand piano on which both Noël Coward and Princess Diana once played.

THE ROYAL TRAIN
Round-Britain express

"There is a perception the Royal Train is a bit like the *Orient Express.* But there are not many furnishings you could not get in Homebase or B&Q."
Tim Hewlett, Director of Royal Travel, 2002

LTHOUGH THE QUEEN sometimes uses scheduled train services for official engagements in the UK, she and the Duke of Edinburgh and the Prince of Wales also have the use of the Royal Train for longer trips around the country. Like *Britannia*, the Royal Train conjures up a picture of journeys conducted in sumptuous luxury. But the reality is rather different. For a start there is no single Royal Train but rather a set of eight carriages fitted out to the specifications of the Queen, Prince Philip and Prince Charles. These are pulled in various combinations (depending on who is travelling and for how long) by either of two identical Class 67 diesel locomotives, *Royal Sovereign* and *Queen's Messenger*, both of which were built in 1999.

Carriage exteriors are painted predominantly 'royal claret' with a grey roof, while the interiors are relatively plain and utilitarian, since the train is designed primarily for royal tours, official engagements and business meetings. The Queen's saloon, which came into service in 1977, is a 75-foot-long carriage consisting of a bedroom, bathroom and sitting room. The small pastel-coloured bedroom is lit by a combination of strip lighting and reading lamps and contains a single bed, bedside table (with a radio) and chair. Her sitting room has an extendable dining table, a desk and a sofa and armchairs. Pictures of Scottish landscapes and selected royal train journeys of the past hang on the walls, and curtains and thick carpets ensure privacy and quiet. Prince Philip's saloon is similar to the Queen's but includes a small kitchen to cater for business lunches. He has a piece of Isambard Kingdom Brunel's original broad gauge rail framed on the wall, along with an enlarged copy of his Senior Railcard, for which he was eligible in 1987.

Royal trains have in fact been in existence since 1842, when Queen Victoria travelled from Slough to Paddington on 13 June. Her train consisted of a saloon and six other carriages and was pulled by the steam engine Phlegethon. In more recent times, the Royal Train came into its own in 1977, whisking the Queen around Britain during her Silver Jubilee, and it is still in constant use.

Journeys on the train are always organised so as not to interfere with scheduled services. Drivers are chosen for their experience and skill and are expected to start and stop the train so smoothly that the royal travellers can barely detect any movement. The train is always halted at nightfall in a secluded siding to give passengers a peaceful night's sleep.

Opposite: The Queen and the young Prince Edward, Prince Andrew and Lady Sarah Armstrong-Jones wave from the window of the Royal Train as it leaves London's Liverpool Street station on 29 December 1971. The royals were travelling to Sandringham House in Norfolk.

Above left: The Queen alighting from the royal train at Liverpool Street with four of her corgis in 1968. Britain's most privileged pets, the corgis also travel by chauffeur-driven limo and private plane or helicopter, and are sometimes carried by Her Majesty's aides.

Above right: During her Golden Jubilee in 2002, the Queen travelled to north Wales in the Royal Train, which on this occasion was drawn by the restored steam locomotive *Duchess of Sutherland*, seen here leaving Llandudno Junction.

THE QUEEN'S PORTRAIT

The Queen has been represented in the visual arts probably more than anyone else in the whole of history. In addition, her face and profile have reached the four corners of the globe on stamps, coins, banknotes and the vast range of memorabilia commemorating the key anniversaries of her reign. Painters ranging from Pietro Annigoni to the Nigerian-born artist Chinwe Chukwuogo-Roy have tried to capture the spirit and warmth of the woman beneath the impersonal royal figure. And photographers such as Dorothy Wilding, Cecil Beaton and Annie Leibovitz have frozen in time classic moments of the Queen's life, from formal state occasions to intimate family gatherings.

PORTRAIT PAINTINGS
A brush with the Queen

The Queen has sat for 140 OFFICIAL PORTRAITS during her lifetime. She was SEVEN years old when she sat for her FIRST PORTRAIT in 1933.

ALTHOUGH HER CHARACTER has largely been a matter of hearsay and speculation, the Queen's face is one of the best known in the world. Throughout her life, more than 130 artists – from Pietro Annigoni and Lucian Freud to Rolf Harris – have tried to capture the essence of her personality through her physical features. Some paintings have proved controversial, but most have presented the Queen as a dignified head of state, elegant and regal, often with a touch of warmth or sense of humour.

Almost all of the Queen's portraits painted by established artists have been commissioned. One notable exception was a screenprint of her created by the American pop artist Andy Warhol in 1985. Warhol based his picture on a photograph of the Queen taken in 1977 for her Silver Jubilee. The print, with its bright candy colours, makes the Queen look like a fresh-faced Hollywood star in an era when the royal family was becoming associated with the prevalent cult of celebrity.

If Warhol's picture seemed daring at the time, it proved to be less controversial than Lucian Freud's painting of the Queen in 2001. Freud, who at that time had claims to be Britain's greatest living painter, was renowned for his naturalism, and he depicted the Queen with a heavily lined face and a severe expression. The

head of the National Portrait Gallery, Charles Saumarez-Smith, described it as "thought-provoking and psychologically penetrating". But Richard Morrison of *The Times* said: "The expression is of a sovereign who has endured not one annus horribilis but an entire reign of them. The Merry Monarch it isn't."

In the following year, the Queen was restored to her full dignity for her Golden Jubilee in a colourful oil painting by the Nigerian-born artist Chinwe Chukwuogo-Roy. The Queen is dressed in a bright royal blue and stands on a red carpet inside Buckingham Palace. Behind her are depicted emblematic images of some of the 54 Commonwealth countries, for example the Taj Mahal for India and Sydney Opera House for Australia.

One of the most surprising choices of artists granted sittings at Buckingham Palace in recent years was, perhaps, Rolf Harris, the Australian-born singer, painter and television presenter. An ardent monarchist, Harris painted the Queen for her 80th birthday in 2006 and based his picture on two sittings at Buckingham Palace. Harris commented: "The portrait I've created aims to capture the Queen's warm and friendly personality, rather than being a very formal portrait."

Far left: The Queen looks delighted after seeing a portrait of herself in Cunard's new cruise ship the *Queen Elizabeth,* which she officially named on 11 October 2010 in Southampton. The picture was commissioned by Cunard and painted by the British artist Isobel Peachey. It shows the Queen sitting in the Yellow Drawing Room at Buckingham Palace wearing Queen Victoria's diamond necklace and earrings, which she also wore at her coronation in 1953.

Left: The first great majestic painting of the Queen after she came to the throne was created by the Italian artist Pietro Annigoni in 1954. He made 15 visits to the palace to paint his subject and found the Queen relaxed and full of conversation, sometimes speaking to him in French. He said of the Queen that "as she posed, her facial expression was mercurial, smiling, thoughtful, determined, uncertain, relaxed, taut, in rapid succession".

PORTRAIT PHOTOGRAPHS
Under the eye of the lens

"The purity of her expression, the unspoilt childishness of the smile, the pristine quality of her pink and white complexion, are all part of an appearance that is individual and gives the effect of a total entity."
Cecil Beaton, 1952

FOR MORE THAN EIGHT DECADES photographers have produced a vast array of images of the Queen, from Dorothy Wilding's early black-and-white classics to Chris Levine's 2004 holographic portrait.

One of the Queen's favourite photographers was Cecil Beaton, who produced an iconic portrait of her as a teenager – looking relaxed in an ATS uniform in 1942. Another photographer to gain privileged access to the Queen early on in her reign was Dorothy Wilding, who also included celebrities such as Noël Coward, George Bernard Shaw and Aldous Huxley among her many subjects. One of Wilding's elegant head-and-shoulders portraits of the Queen became the model for her image on British stamps.

Other iconic photographs of the Queen down the years have included Eve Arnold's 1968 shot of her holding a black umbrella and staring up at the grey skies with a broad smile on her face, and Patrick Lichfield's 1971 informal snap of her relaxed and laughing on board *Britannia* as she watches someone being thrown overboard in jest. Lord Snowdon, the husband of Princess Margaret, produced a luminous portrait of her beaming with pleasure as she held her baby grandson, Peter Phillips, in 1977. And in 2007 the American

photographer Annie Leibovitz created a portrait of the Queen so rich in colour and detail it looks almost like a painting: the Queen is sitting in the White Drawing Room at Buckingham Palace, gazing through an open window and attired in a pale gold evening dress, fur stole and diamond tiara.

One of the most unusual recent portraits of the Queen was Chris Levine's 2004 shot 'Lightness of Being', which shows her sitting up, wearing her crown and royal finery, but with her eyes shut. Levine had been photographing her for a holographic portrait, for which each exposure took eight seconds. He asked the Queen to relax between shots and was able to capture her with her eyes closed.

Left: The Queen looks relaxed in an official 80th birthday portrait that captures the tenderness of the nation's 'favourite grandmother'. It is by photographer Jane Bown, famous for her iconic images of Bertrand Russell, Mick Jagger and Samuel Beckett.

Right: Swathed in a turquoise, the young Queen looks like a character from an opera in this Cecil Beaton photograph taken in the 1950s. Cecil Beaton photographed the Queen as a teenage princess, as a newly crowned Queen, and as a young and devoted mother.

PORTRAIT SCULPTURES
Set in bronze and stone

Left: The Queen unveils a portrait bust of herself by Oscar Nemon at the House of Lords on 20 October 2009. The bust is one-and-quarter life size and rests on an octagonal oak pedestal. It is displayed in the Robing Room in the Palace of Westminster.

Right: The Queen walks past a statue of herself riding her favourite horse, Burmese, in Regina, Saskatchewan, after she had unveiled it on 18 May 2005. It was created by the Canadian sculptor Susan Velder to mark the Golden Jubilee. The Queen had ridden Burmese for 18 consecutive Trooping the Colours, from 1969 to 1986.

ALTHOUGH PAINTINGS AND PHOTOGRAPHS of the Queen have been legion, sculptures and statues of her are much fewer in number. However, over the years the Queen has been modelled in sand at the Weston-super-Mare Sand Sculpture Festival, carved into a bronze bas-relief for the newly opened Supreme Court, and cast in the form of a bronze bust for the House of Lords. The bust was created from a plaster original made in the 1960s by the late Croatian sculptor Oscar Nemon and which was unearthed in the artist's attic after his death in 1985.

The only statue of the Queen in the United Kingdom is in Windsor Great Park. Fashioned from two and a half tonnes of bronze, the statue was created by the British sculptor Philip Jackson for the Golden Jubilee in 2002. It shows the Queen on horseback – as if she had just ridden up Queen Anne's Ride and had stopped to gaze back at Windsor Castle. The same Jubilee was also the spur for another equestrian statue of the Queen – in Saskatchewan in Canada. It shows her riding her favourite horse, Burmese, which had been presented to her by the Royal Canadian Mounted Police back in 1969. On 9 December 2010 a carved corbel of the Queen was unveiled in the foyer of the Canadian Senate, "a reminder of the high esteem in which Canadians hold Her Majesty."

"I think the Queen would show her dislike of something in a very subtle way. I was standing next to her when it was unveiled, and prior to the unveiling one of the equerries said she would be very embarrassed about it. I was slightly taken aback and he said, well, actually, she's a very modest woman."

Sculptor Philip Jackson on the unveiling of his equestrian statue of the Queen in Windsor Great Park in 2002.

STAMPS AND MONEY

In our hearts and pockets

THE QUEEN'S HEAD has adorned British and Commonwealth money and stamps since her coronation. From British shillings and pence to Canadian cents and Australian dollars, her profile has literally been in the pockets of millions of people. And her face or silhouette has traversed the globe on the stamps of countless letters and parcels.

The history of monarchs' heads appearing on coins in England goes back to Anglo-Saxon times and the likes of King Offa of Mercia and Alfred the Great. Since the 17th century the sovereign's head has been shown in profile, and the direction it faces traditionally alternates with each successive reign. The Queen's head always faces to the right and her successor's will face the left.

When British coins received a complete facelift with the decimalisation of the currency in 1971, the Queen's image appeared in a new design by the sculptor Arnold Machin. Updated depictions of her were introduced in 1985, 1998, 2007 and 2012. Her image can be found on banknotes too – there have been five different depictions of her during her reign – but, unlike on the coins, her face is more of a frontal portrait facing the left.

The Queen's head also appears on British stamps – a tradition that started in 1840 when Queen Victoria's head appeared on the Penny Black. The first image of Queen Elizabeth to appear on the corners of British letters was based on a photograph by Dorothy Wilding. The image lasted from 1952 to 1967, when a new profile created by Arnold Machin and usually set on a single colour, was introduced. The Machin series, as it is known, is still in use, and on its 40th anniversary in 2007, the Post Office issued a stamp featuring a photograph of Machin himself.

Only twice in the Queen's reign has there been any talk of removing her head from stamps. In 1965 the Labour Postmaster-General Tony Benn tried for a while to persuade the Queen that the design of the stamps would be improved by their being 'headless'. The Queen listened politely but in the end her head remained. Benn commented afterwards: "I could foresee that if these [headless] stamps were published … this would be presented as the final straw: 'Benn knocks Queen off stamps'." Then in 2011, there was speculation in the press that possible government plans to sell off Royal Mail might result in a foreign buyer removing the Queen's head from stamps, even though the Postal Affairs minister Ed Davey commented that any buyer would be "mad" to drop it.

Far left: The Royal Mail issued a set of stamps to commemorate the Queen's 60th birthday in 1986. They show photographs of her taken in each decade of her life.

Centre: The Queen's portrait on Bank of England banknotes has changed throughout her reign. A one pound note (top) designed by Robert Austin and issued on 17 March 1960 was the first note to carry a portrait of the Queen. Below this one, the other notes were produced in 1963 (designed by Reynolds Stone); 1970 (Harry Ecclestone); 1971 (Harry Ecclestone); and 1990 (Roger Withington). On banknotes the Queen's head always faces left, but with a hidden watermark showing her looking to the right.

Left: The Queen's head always faces to the right on British and Commonwealth coins, as these four examples show. The coins carry a Latin inscription, 'Elizabeth II Dei Gratia Regina Fidei Defensor' (often abbreviated to Elizabeth II D G Reg F D), which means 'Elizabeth II, by the grace of God, Queen and Defender of the Faith'.

CHINA AND MEMORABILIA
Royal souvenirs

Royal memorabilia can be TRACED BACK *to* 1660, *when a* COMMEMORATIVE MUG *was produced to mark Charles II's* RESTORATION *to the throne.*

THROUGHOUT HER REIGN the Queen has inspired a veritable industry in memorabilia bearing her image. From mugs, plates, spoons and medals to figurines, tins and T-shirts, her face has launched a thousand souvenirs, especially during her jubilee years.

The production of royal souvenirs dates back to the 17th century, but manufacturers were allowed to use the monarch's image on their products only after the coronation of George II in 1727. Memorabilia of the Queen herself began in earnest in 1953, when many local councils marked her coronation by commissioning potteries to make commemorative mugs to give away to local children. A wide range of items bearing the Queen's image were mass-produced in the coronation year, ranging from tins of biscuits and tea caddies to handkerchiefs and flags.

In the same year, Wedgwood produced an elegant mug showing the Queen's profile in blue relief on a white background, while Royal Doulton created a fine bone-china tankard with a photographic portrait of the Queen, semi-framed by an oak branch. This was the last commemorative item to come out of the Doulton factory in Lambeth, London, and has become a valuable collector's item.

Producers of memorabilia were given another major shot in the arm with the Silver Jubilee in 1977. At the high end of the market, Royal Worcester produced a formal blue plate decorated in the centre by the royal coat of arms in gold on a white background. At the more commercial end, Cadbury's brought out a handsome Milk Tray chocolates tin, with the portraits of the Queen and Prince Philip appearing on a rich mauve background. Carr's sold an Assorted Biscuits tin, adorned with a photograph of a smiling Queen sitting on a gold-covered chair. More unusual was an Umbro football shirt made up of an array of colours to reflect the different clubs in the Glasgow area who formed a team to play a Jubilee celebration match.

The Golden Jubilee in 2002 proved no different as a souvenir-spawner, and there was the usual range of goods. Royalists could eat their toast from a classic gold-and-blue Spode plate with a portrait of the Queen, or nibble on Walkers shortbread biscuits from a tin decorated with an image of the Queen superimposed on a gold-coloured map of the world and ringed with flags of the Commonwealth countries. And they could pour their Earl Grey from a James Sadler teapot with its gold silhouette of the Queen, and stir in the milk with a Royal Mint silver teaspoon.

Far left: A tea caddy adorned with the Queen's portrait, the Union Jack and the Australian national flag, was produced to commemorate the Queen's visit to Australia in 1954.

Above: This selection of souvenirs shows the range of objects produced for the Queen's coronation – from tankards, bone china teacups and silver napkin rings and spoons to pens, model figures and engraved crystal drinking glasses. There is even a delicate silver model of the State Coach.

Right: This teacup and saucer, with the Queen's head framed by the Union Jack and the Royal Standard, is typical of the chinaware made to commemorate royal anniversaries and special occasions.

QUEEN ON THE SCREEN

The televising of the Queen's coronation in 1953 was recognised as a milestone
in the history of broadcasting, and just four years later the Queen's Christmas
broadcast was televised for the first time. As the new medium became an established
fact of life, the public began to feel entitled to a degree of access to the royal
family's private, as well as their ceremonial, lives. A succession of documentaries
have attempted, with varying degrees of success, to paint a comprehensive picture
of the Queen – some traditionalists fear that they have merely served to whet
the public's appetite for gossip and revelation. At the same time, the Queen has
exerted an enduring fascination for film-makers, and has been depicted by a range
of leading actresses.

THE QUEEN'S SPEECH
Christmas broadcasts

"It is inevitable that I should seem a rather remote figure to many of you… now at least for a few minutes I welcome you to the peace of my own home."

First televised broadcast, 1957

WIRELESS BROADCASTS to the Empire each Christmas started in 1932 at the suggestion of Sir John Reith, founding father of the BBC, when the Queen's grandfather King George V spoke to 20 million people from Sandringham on Christmas day, opening with the words, "I speak now from my home and from my heart to you all." It was only with the war years that the Christmas broadcast became an entrenched tradition. The Queen's father, King George VI, overcoming nervousness and a severe stammer, broadcast regularly to the nation, asserting his belief in the common cause they were fighting for and boosting public morale during the darkest days of the Blitz.

On her father's death the Queen took over the traditional Christmas duty, even broadcasting from the same desk and chair that her father had used, a mark of respect for her much loved predecessor. Every year of her reign – except 1969, when the documentary *Royal Family* was broadcast – the Queen has honoured this tradition. Just four years after her coronation, in 1957, she gave the first televised Christmas message. This allowed millions of viewers actually to see the Queen in her home environment – normally Buckingham Palace, but some times Sandringham or Windsor – and many eager subjects pored over visual clues, from her Christmas tree to her displays of cards, with keen interest.

The Christmas broadcast is one of the rare occasions when the Queen does not turn to the Government for advice, but voices her own views, reflecting current issues. Frequent preoccupations have been the importance of the family, the role of the Commonwealth and the predicament of the armed forces, fighting battles and endangering their lives in the remote corners of the globe. The format of the speech has evolved over the years to include edited footage of royal events throughout the year. From 1960 the actual speech was pre-recorded some ten days before the broadcast, and copies of the tape were sent to Commonwealth countries around the world. Today, despite the innovations of internet and on-demand broadcasting, the speech is always transmitted at 3pm on Christmas afternoon.

The speech normally lasts about ten minutes, and attracts between 5 and 10 million domestic viewers. The home audience reached its pinnacle in 1993, the year after the Queen's 'Annus Horribilis' speech, when it numbered 21 million. The Queen is said to avoid watching the speech with the family, but scrutinises it in her own private room.

Far left: The Queen makes her first Christmas Day broadcast in 1952 from Sandringham House. She opened the speech with an explicit link to the past, emphasising the contintuity of tradition: "Each Christmas, at this time, my beloved father broadcast a message to his people in all parts of the world …As he used to do, I am speaking to you from my own home, where I am spending Christmas with my family."

Left: A London family looks at the Queen's first televised Christmas broadcast to the British people in 1957. The Queen had been very nervous about appearing on television, and had confessed that her Christmas had been ruined by the looming broadcast, which was transmitted live.

ROYAL FAMILY 1969
Daylight on the magic

"The whole institution depends on mystique and the tribal chief in his hut. If any member of the tribe ever sees inside the hut, then the whole system of the tribal chiefdom is damaged and the tribe eventually disintegrates."
David Attenborough

AN ATTEMPT TO DEMYSTIFY the monarchy and allow the British public to get to know their royal family, the groundbreaking 1969 documentary, simply entitled *Royal Family*, was always controversial. The Queen Mother was opposed to its production, saying it was "a terrible idea", and the Queen was reluctant to give her consent. Eventually, she ordered that the film should be removed from circulation, and her attitude to the film remains implacably negative.

The Queen's press secretary William Heseltine, Lord Mountbatten (Prince Philip's uncle) and the television producer Lord Brabourne, who was Lord Mountbatten's son-in-law, were all firmly convinced that the public would love this insight into royal family life; the nation would take this 'ordinary family' to their hearts. But in the end, many commentators felt that the demystification of the monarchy had started a slow slide into tabloid journalism, celebrity culture, media revelations and a general lack of respect.

Director Richard Cawston was given unparalleled access to the Queen, and shot 43 hours of raw footage of the Queen's private and official life. The final product was edited down to 105 minutes, and was aired to BBC audiences of 40 million

on 21 June 1969, just before Prince Charles's investiture at Caernarvon Castle. The cameras recorded the Queen going about her personal business, recording her small talk with world leaders. More intrusively, they eavesdropped on a highly contrived family barbecue at Balmoral, showing the Queen and Prince Charles making a salad, while Prince Philip and Princess Anne grilled sausages. Prince Philip reminisced about his eccentric father-in-law, who used to wear a bearskin and hack away at the rhododendrons in the royal garden, all the time venting a string of foul language. Edward bickered with Charles, while the Queen told amusing anecdotes about her illustrious forebears.

The Queen comes across as cheerful, hard-working, dutiful, and endearingly old-fashioned. The family seem happy and united, enjoying the life of the British upper classes, surrounded by horses, dogs and servants. The public watched the documentary with voyeuristic pleasure, but were not taken in by attempts to 'package' the royal family as ordinary. The public appetite had been whetted, and daylight had certainly been let in on the royal magic. The Queen had allowed the media unprecedented access to her private life, but she was soon to find that she had created a monster with a limitless appetite for royal stories and, ultimately, scandals.

Far left: Queen Elizabeth II and Prince Philip look at their decorated Christmas tree during the filming of a television special about life in the British royal family. The public were fascinated by every aspect of the Queen's life, from the decorations she chose for her Christmas tree to her recipe for salad dressing.

Above: Cameras film a family lunch at Windsor Castle, with the Queen, Prince Philip, Princess Anne and Prince Charles. Elizabeth, who never enjoyed the formal filming of the Christmas broadcast, was remarkably at ease on camera. All aspects of her life were filmed, from riding in the country, to choosing her outfits for an upcoming state visit and receiving newly-appointed ambassadors at St. James's Palace.

The 'fly-on-the-wall' camera made social occasions appear contrived, however, and family conversations were highly stilted. The film was seen as a golden opportunity to promote the next generation, but Prince Charles in particular, came across as traditional, old-fashioned and out of touch, with his tweed jackets, neatly trimmed hair and deferential manners. The young royals seemed very far removed from their contemporaries, who were enjoying unparalleled freedom in 1960s London.

LIFE IN THE SPOTLIGHT
A continuing fascination

IN 1992 DOCUMENTARY-PRODUCER and director Edward Mirzoeff was commissioned to make *Elizabeth R*, a 110-minute portrait of the life of the monarch, marking the 40th anniversary of her accession to the throne. Over the course of a year he followed the Queen as she went about her usual business: access to the monarch was controlled and stage-managed, and there was no chink of revelation to satisfy more voyeuristic viewers.

The intent was to create a positive, reverential picture of the monarch, and the documentary certainly did so. But critics felt that, at a time when the royal family was going through a period of turmoil, the film was not revealing enough. The 1969 documentary had let the genie out of the bottle, and the public were eager for more.

In 2007 the BBC screened a five-part series named *Monarchy: The Royal Family at Work,* with Denys Blakeway as executive producer. Once again cameras recorded the Queen at work, and once again she came across as a hard-working and consummate professional, adept at small talk and confidently putting powerful (and nervous) men at their ease. There were few revelations, but small details, like the Queen's taste for gin and dubonnet in a 70:30 ratio, fascinated viewers.

The Queen has been a media innovator throughout her reign.

In 1976 the Queen became the first monarch to send an email during a visit to an army base. She launched the royal website in 1997 on a visit to Kingsbury High School in Brent.

In 2006 her Christmas broadcast was podcast for the first time, and in 2007 the Queen launched the first Royal Channel on YouTube. In 2010 the Queen even launched an official Facebook page.

Top left: The Queen on a walkabout was a focus for film-makers in 2007, who charted her everyday life in *Monarchy: the Royal Family at Work*. As well as state occasions and meetings with heads of state, the cameras recorded some of the more personal moments in her daily life. Film-makers went behind the scenes at a state banquet in Tallinn, where organisers fretted that flower arrangements might provoke a royal sneezing attack. There was also a scene when an air crew were briefed about the requirements of the Queen and Prince Philip, which include a well-mixed gin and dubonnet, and a range of newspapers, including the Queen's favourite *Racing Post*.

Above: The Queen and Queen Mother do their best to enjoy horse-racing, while ignoring the close proximity of a BBC camera and sound-boom. This was just one scene in Ed Mirzoeff's *Elizabeth R*, a film that diligently tracked the Queen over the course of a year (1992), as a celebration of her 40 years on the throne.

CELLULOID QUEEN
Depictions in movies and television

"She was constant, she never wavered, she's gone on through fashions, politics, nine or ten prime ministers. She has continued – an amazing quality to have in this time that isn't about continuum."
Helen Mirren on the Queen

Depictions of the Queen on film have undergone a fundamental change since Herbert Wilcox's reverential movies on the life of Victoria, *Victoria the Great* and *Sixty Glorious Years*, starring his future wife Anna Neagle, were launched in 1937. When, in 1965, an American documentary-maker produced *A King's Story*, narrated by Orson Welles, in which the Duke and Duchess of Windsor narrated their own account of the abdication crisis, the floodgates were opened and an enduring fascination was born.

To some extent precipitated by the in-depth documentary, *Royal Family* (1969), the Queen found herself and her relations the focus of film-makers' fascination. The drama of the abdication crisis continues to attract film-makers, most notably *The King's Speech* (2010), which won the Oscar for best picture in 2011. Prince Charles's marriage became a kind of soap opera, the subject of an American made-for-television film, *Charles and Diana: A Royal Love Story*. With the collapse of the marriage, the knives were out, and the Queen was forced to endure *Charles and Camilla – Whatever Love Means*. The Queen herself has been the target of satirists (most controversially in *Spitting Image*, where her latex puppet was voiced by Jan Ravens), dramatists and documentary-makers. She has been played by a great range of actresses, including Margaret Tyzack, Prunella Scales, Rosemary Leach, Juliet Aubrey and Helen Mirren.

The Queen (2006), starring Helen Mirren, was an acclaimed feature film, directed by Stephen Frears, with a plot that hinged on the critical week after the death of Princess Diana, when the Queen and her close family withdrew to the privacy of Balmoral, and did not fully understand the public grief that had the rest of the country in its grip. Prime Minister Tony Blair seeks to interpret the public mood to the Queen, and eventually they reach a mutual understanding.

Mirren spent many hours looking at footage of the Queen, and came up with an uncannily accurate interpretation. In an interview, Mirren commented: "she won't perform or act something she doesn't feel. Her job is to be dignified, gracious, but above all serious…She has two kinds of smile. There's her formal smile, and sometimes a genuine smile and you can tell she's enjoying herself, engaged."

Helen Mirren won an Oscar for her performance. Avowed monarchists were unhappy about the portrayal of a reigning monarch on the screen, especially in such a high profile film.

Far left: Prunella Scales played the Queen in Alan Bennett's play *A Question of Attribution*, which was staged at the National Theatre in 1988, along with a companion piece called *An Englishman Abroad*. The two plays were amalgamated into *Single Spies*, which was screened on the BBC in 1992. The play focuses on Anthony Blunt, the Surveyor of the Queen's Pictures, who was uncovered as a member of the Cambridge Spy Ring. It examines his attitude to art and betrayal and his relationship with the Queen. Prunella Scales was commended for her portayal of a monarch who mixed genuine inquisitiveness and curiosity with icy shrewdness.

Left: Helen Mirren in Stephen Frears' film *The Queen* (2006). Although the film was essentially a docudrama, combining real reported incidents with fiction and speculation, nobody questioned the extraordinary accuracy of Mirren's interpretation: "It took no time at all to become her," she commented. "The wig helped. The big glasses helped. The way the head is held is very distinctive… I do look a bit like her, you know…"

THE QUEEN'S IMAGE

One of the most famous women in the world, the Queen is well used to the closest scrutiny and analysis. She has evolved, publicly, from a wasp-waisted, glamorous princess to a stately and elegant elder stateswoman and her distinctive style has served her well. From the earliest years of her reign she realised that her clothes were both symbolic and diplomatic. A simple choice of colour could signify a recognition of nationalist sensibilities; an emblematic brooch, or intricate embroidered design, could indicate respect for a host nation. The Queen accepts that she is not just a woman, she is a figurehead, and her appearance is, therefore, truly iconic.

NORMAN HARTNELL
Lavish glamour

"I thought of altar cloths and sacred vestments; I thought of the sky, the earth, the sun, the moon, the stars and everything heavenly that might be embroidered on a dress destined to be historic."
Norman Hartnell

GLAMOROUS, ROMANTIC, intricately wrought, Norman Hartnell's designs for the Queen were the epitome of court fashion. A truly British couturier, who eschewed the fashionable allure of Paris, Hartnell was notable for designing the two most important dresses of the Queen's ceremonial life – her wedding dress and her coronation gown.

Born in 1901, Norman Hartnell began his creative career when he was a student at Cambridge, and he began designing theatrical costumes. He turned professional, and opened his London salon in 1923. His early collections focused on tailored day wear and elegant evening dresses. But his royal connections were to propel him to fame. His breakthrough came when he was commissioned to design the bride's and bridesmaids' dresses for the wedding of the Duke of Gloucester, third son of King George V. The Princesses Elizabeth and Margaret were two of the bridesmaids.

By the 1930s Hartnell was designing for Queen Elizabeth. His feminine, pastel confections were inspired by the romantic paintings of the Victorian court painter Franz Winterhalter. It was King George VI's express wish that his wife's clothes would offer a captivating counterpoint to the brittle glamour of

Wallis Simpson. Hartnell's floating designs for the royal tour of Paris in 1938 were a triumph, and he was commissioned to create Princess Elizabeth's 1947 wedding dress. Inspired by Botticelli, the satin dress shimmered with embroidered garlands of seed pearls and crystals. In post-war austerity Britain, Hartnell's creation was a sensation.

Hartnell's next landmark was Queen Elizabeth's coronation gown. Modelled on the Queen's wedding gown in white satin, Hartnell used silk, pearls and diamante to create a symbolic, embroidered tribute to both her kingdom and her dominions. He went on to design the Queen's wardrobe for her landmark 1953 Coronation Tour. Lasting six months, the Queen would require over 100 outfits, suitable for a range of climates. Hartnell's magnificent collection made liberal use of crease-resistant duchesse satin and his trademark elaborate embroidery. The sumptuous dresses were freighted with symbolic significance, each paying a tribute – in either the colour or the design – to the country she was visiting.

Hartnell's stately court dresses were eventually eclipsed by the more democratic fashions of the 1960s. His legacy of majestic, fairytale dresses define the early decades of the Queen's reign.

Opposite left: For the 1970 tour of Australia Hartnell created a daringly short bright mimosa-yellow day dress and matching coat that could be accessorised with the yellow-diamond wattle brooch the Queen was given by the Australian people and a light straw Simone Mirman hat.

Opposite right: A dress fit for a new Queen. This Norman Hartnell-designed one-shoulder gown in the crinoline style was made in 1953. The glamorous evening dress was made of gold lamé overlaid with lace and embroidered with gold thread.

Left: The ultimate accolade for Norman Hartnell was his commission to design the Queen's coronation dress. He submitted eight different designs each developing the complex symbolism of Commonwealth motifs that were to be embroidered into the fabric of the dress. The white satin used to make the dress was obtained from Lady Hart Dyke's silk farm at Lullingstone Castle. Six embroideresses worked in utmost secrecy. The finished gown was delivered to the Palace three days before the coronation and the Queen pronouced it "glorious".

HARDY AMIES
Nonchalant elegance

"The best-dressed woman is one whose clothes wouldn't look too strange in the country."
Sir Hardy Amies

HARDY AMIES STARTED designing for the Queen in the early 1950s and retired at the age of 93 in 2003. He was a masterful tailor, who guided the Queen towards the sharper silhouettes of the 1960s and 1970s. In fact, in the 1950s, recognising the need for cheaper, stylish clothes Hardy Amies expanded his business to open a ready-to-wear boutique and designed for many High Street labels. He claimed to be realistic, rather than romantic, about fashion.

Hardy Amies did not have a fashion background, and aspired to be a journalist. His facility with words, and his vivid description of a dress, brought him to the attention of the Mayfair couture house Lachasse, and by the 1930s he was designing the whole collection. After some daredevil wartime experiences in the Special Operations Executive, he opened his own fashion house in Savile Row.

He soon came to the attention of royal circles, and was asked to design Princess Elizabeth's wardrobe for her visit to Canada in 1948; his royal warrant dates from her accession to the throne. He developed a close relationship with the Queen, visiting Buckingham Palace several times a year for fittings. His success as a royal dressmaker was in many ways

due to the attention he paid to the Queen's very particular demands. Skirts must not be too short so they don't ride up when she sits down; jackets must be buttoned, so they don't fall open when she waves. Hems of dresses are often weighted, to avoid blowing around in the wind. The Queen cannot wear dark colours because she will look like she's in mourning; beige is too neutral and invisible, especially given the Queen's diminutive 5ft 3in-stature. This is why the Queen tends to wear blocks of strong colour – aquamarines, fuschia pinks, daffodil yellow.

Hardy Amies's accomplished tailoring makes his outfits look deceptively simple. In fact, the Queen's grey satin full-skirted gown, exquisitely decorated with a fern motif in bugle beads, crystal and pearl, which she wore in 1957 at a dinner given for her at the White House, was as intricately worked as any of Hartnell's creations. Other notable outfits designed by Hardy Amies include a turquoise-blue shift made for the state visit to Germany in 1965, and decorated with silver embroidery. The Queen wore a pink silk dress and coat for the Silver Jubilee and a Hardy Amies yellow coat on her 60th birthday. In the words of Hardy Amies, "I do not dress the Queen, the Queen dresses herself. We supply her with clothes – there is a difference."

Above left: works in progress – two sketches by Hardy Amies for a wedding outfit (left) and an outfit for the royal tour of South Africa (right). The finished clothes can be seen in the photographs above.

Above: The Queen wears a Hardy Amies-designed lilac knee-length coat, with a matching floral day dress and lilac hat for the wedding of Crown Prince Pavlos of Greece in 1995. She is accompanied by King Hussein of Jordan and Prince Philip.

Above: The Queen arrives at City Hall, Durban, during her 1995 state visit to South Africa. She is wearing a flowing floral dress and matching jacket by Hardy Amies, in a striking multicoloured flower pattern on a yellow background.

IAN THOMAS
Sophisticated ease

Left: Sketch of a fishtail body-hugging evening dress, created for Queen Elizabeth II by fashion designer Ian Thomas. The dress was worn to a gala performance in Covent Garden, London, in 1979.

Below: The Queen, on a visit to Blois in France in 1992, wears a pink and taupe outfit designed by Ian Thomas.

Right: A sketch of a short-sleeved aquamarine dress, with matching pleated coat, and hat, all designed by Ian Thomas for the wedding, in 1981, of Prince Charles and Lady Diana Spencer.

A PROTÉGÉ OF HARDY AMIES, Ian Thomas was an unassuming designer whose other main passion was riding and showing hunters. He was a class winner at the Royal Windsor Horse Show. After graduating from Oxford College of Art in 1952, he assisted Norman Hartnell with the embroidery on the coronation robes, and continued this tradition of intricate workmanship when he founded his own fashion house in 1969.

He dressed not only the Queen, but many high society ladies. They came to him for his restrained elegance and the relaxed style of his flowing chiffon dresses, which captured the more fluid fashions of the 1970s. He made the Queen both day clothes and glamorous dresses for grand occasions. In 2011 his white short-sleeved evening dress, worn by the Queen for President Ceaucescu of Romania's state visit to London in 1978, was displayed in Ireland before the Queen's visit.

One of his finest creations was designed for the Queen's tour of Australia in 1974. The yellow evening dress and cape of bright yellow silk-chiffon, embroidered with sprays of wattle, the national flower of Australia, was not worn as the Queen had to return early to England when a general election was called. The dress was later worn on several state occasions.

Ian Thomas 1981

STEWART PARVIN
Elegant understatement

Stewart Parvin is the youngest of the Queen's designers. He was commissioned over a decade ago to refresh the Queen's wardrobe and give her a new look. He submitted sketches and swatches, and the Queen chose five outfits including her famous pale blue cobweb lace dress which has been seen on many occasions and featured in a Buckingham Palace exhibition. He has been called upon to design the clothes for many grand state occasions, and has also been very successful in creating Ascot outfits for the Queen, that are striking, fresh and pretty.

Stewart Parvin trained at the Edinburgh College of Art, and went on to work for the acclaimed couturier Donald Campbell. He set up his own label in 1995, creating two collections a year. In 2007 he was awarded the Royal Warrant of Appointment to Her Majesty the Queen in recognition of his work.

2011 was a milestone year for Stewart Parvin. He designed a very high profile white evening dress for the Queen, which she wore during the state visit of President Barack Obama. He also created a beautiful duchesse satin wedding dress, with a full skirt and fitted bodice, for the Queen's granddaughter Zara Phillips.

Far left: The Queen wore a striking Stewart Parvin outfit in vibrant red when she visited her grandson Prince William at his Sea King helicopter base in Anglesey, Wales, in April 2011.

Left: The Queen wore Stewart Parvin when she stepped out onto Irish soil on her state visit in May 2011. Seen here with Prince Philip and Tánaiste (deputy prime minister) and foreign affairs minister Eamon Gilmore on their arrival at Baldonnel Airport, the Queen is wearing a striking jade green dress and matching coat by Stewart Parvin and a hat by Rachel Trevor-Morgan. As a tribute to her hosts, green was a predominant colour in her wardrobe on this visit.

Opposite left: The Queen enjoys Royal Ascot in 2009, wearing a predominantly yellow outfit by Stewart Parvin. The floral yellow dress is set off by a fitted three-buttoned yellow jacket and matching hat. Bookmakers William Hill took bets on the colour of the Queen's hat for Ladies' Day, with yellow the favourite at 4/1.

ANGELA KELLY

Trusted advice

Left: The Queen wears a military style creation by Angela Kelly as she attends an equestrian event involving horse racing, cavalry displays and horsemanship skills at the Royal Cavalry Show Ground in Muscat, Oman, in November 2010.

ONCE THE QUEEN'S DRESSER, Liverpudlian Angela Kelly has become indispensable. She now holds the lofty title of Personal Assistant, Adviser and Curator to Her Majesty the Queen (Jewellery, Insignias and Wardrobe). She is entirely responsible for the way the Queen looks in public, not only organising her complete wardrobe and liaising with dressmakers and designers, but now designing her clothes as well.

Angela Kelly, who had met the Queen while she was working for the British Ambassador to Germany in 1992, became one of the Queen's dressers in 1993. She soon rose through the ranks and the Queen invited her to listen to her conversations with designers such as Sir Hardy Amies. When the Queen asked for her opinion, Angela Kelly did not hesitate to give it, and the Queen grew to like and trust the forthright Liverpudlian.

Angela Kelly began to design outfits for the Queen, which were created by Alison Pordum, the Queen's Dressmaker, who worked in-house with Angela Kelly, until Christmas 2008. Kelly has been credited, over the last decade, with an elegant renaissance in the Queen's wardrobe. Old fashioned turban hats and a range of clothes in pastel sweet pea colours

have been swept aside, and the Queen's wardrobe has been rejuvenated with signature colour blocks, chic tailoring, striking accessories and a sharp eye for detail.

This transition was very evident in 2011. The Queen wore Angela Kelly for her grandson William's marriage to Kate Middleton. Her single crepe wool primrose dress (*right*), with hand-sewn beading at the neck in the shape of sunrays, and matching double crepe wool tailored primrose coat won universal praise. Kelly also designed the Queen's hat – in matching crepe with hand-made silk roses and apricot-coloured leaves. The Queen re-wore the dress and hat, without the coat, on her state visit to Canberra, Australia, in 2011. Angela Kelly was also the mastermind behind the Queen's much-lauded wardrobe on her historic state visit to Ireland in May 2011. She ensured that a green-hued palette predominated, in honour of the Queen's hosts.

Angela Kelly is admired for her thrift and is adept at remodelling dresses. In 2009 she took the Queen's favourite evening dress, removed the appliqués of local birds and flowers that had adorned it for a state visit to Trinidad, and substituted crystal maple leaves in preparation for a state visit to Canada the following year.

HATS
The crowning glory

GROWING UP IN AN ERA when hats were *de rigueur* for ladies, the Queen has continued to wear hats throughout her lifetime. Her hats have acted as both a shield and an enhancement – they flatter her face, complement her clothes, and make her stand out in the crowd. One of her milliners, Simone Mirman, once said "Designing for the Queen is always about the whole outfit."

Simone Mirman, a French emigrée who had run the millinery department at the French couturier Elsa Schiaparelli, came to the Queen's attention when she started making hats for Norman Hartnell. She had succeeded in bringing French flair and ingenuity to rationed wartime Britain and had become much sought after in society circles. She was eventually granted royal warrants by the Queen Mother and Princess Margaret as well as the Queen.

Mirman became known as 'the queen of turbans', making that idiosyncratic style her own. But she clearly understood the Queen's millinery requirements: as one of the most photographed women in the world, the Queen chose hats to suit the camera. The brims were never allowed to conceal her face, and for that reason berets, pillbox hats, turban-shaped hats and hats with upturned brims have always been popular. The crowns were designed to protect her carefully set hair, the style and colour had to match her outfits (she never wears hats in a contrasting colour), and the materials had to be striking and memorable.

Australian-born Freddie Fox came to the Queen's attention when Hardy Amies asked him to design five hats for a royal tour in 1968. He said: "I got her head measurements from the vendeuse at Hardy Amies and made the hats myself with a stamp stuck on my desk." He eventually met the Queen for a fitting, and later recalled his nervousness: "When it was time to leave I knew I had to back out but the room was so full of furniture and corgis I was scared I would trip." He was granted a royal warrant and went on to design more than 350 hats for the Queen over a period of 34 years.

Phillip Somerville, from New Zealand, began designing hats for the Queen under Ian Thomas's label and, from 1988, under his own name. He became a royal warrant-holder in 1994. According to Somerville: "The main thing is the hat has to stay on in any calamity, wind or rain, without the Queen having to hold it on. I have to make certain it sits on and stays on. I usually use two hat-pins. The Queen told me once she had never lost a hat."

Far left: Simone Mirman was commissioned to design the hat the Queen wore for the investiture of her son, Charles, Prince of Wales, in 1969. This modification of an early Tudor headdress was a perfect accompaniment to her beige and gold collarless coat, and became an instant classic.

Above: The punters at Royal Ascot are increasingly forsaking the horses on Ladies' Day and betting instead on the design of the Queen's hat. In 2008 bookmaker William Hill reported an above average backing for the fascinator, while other race-goers ventured bets on the colour of the Queen's hat, with Paddy Power slashing the odds on red from 20-1 to 1-3 following a rush of bets. In the event, the Queen opted to wear a pastel blue hat by Philip Somerville, a perfect colour match for her Stewart Parvin dress and coat.

Above: The Queen in the Solomon Isles during her official tour of the South Pacific Islands in 1974 wearing a Freddie Fox turban-style hat in a polka dot fabric that matches her dress, with exuberant asymmetric feathers framing her face.

SCARVES, GLOVES AND HANDBAGS
Finishing touches

Left: The Queen favours a boxy, top-fastening style of handbag that can be held comfortably over her arm. It is said that if the bag is dangling comfortably from her left arm Her Majesty is at ease.

Opposite: The Queen, in a striking fuchsia, black and white headscarf, presents prizes at Queens Cup Polo, Windsor.

ENJOYING HER COUNTRY RETREATS at Balmoral, Windsor and Sandringham, the Queen is often to be seen in a headscarf and tweed skirt. She was even portrayed on a 1956 postage stamp wearing a Hermès scarf. A short, square scarf, tied securely under her chin, is a practical accessory for country walks and equestrian events, and the Queen has also – on occasion – worn longer, flowing varieties. On a visit to a mosque in Turkey, she wore a fine flowing length of silk indicating her respect, and was nicknamed 'the Queen of Scarves' by a British newspaper.

Another indispensable feature of the Queen's wardrobe is the inevitable pair of gloves. These are frequently crisp and white, or a dark-toned leather that matches her handbag. In the evening she wears long opera gloves that extend to just above the elbow.

The final accessory that complements the Queen's myriad outfits is the small handbag, invariably held over the crook of her arm, and always matching her shoes and outfit. The London-based handbag-makers Launer hold the royal warrant. After the Queen appeared at Prince William's wedding carrying a boxy, top-handled cream calfskin handbag from Launer, they experienced a 60 per cent boom in sales.

The Queen's handbag does not contain money, credit cards or a mobile phone, but is useful for carrying her makeup compact (a wedding gift from Prince Philip), a camera, handkerchief, mints and crosswords.

When dining out the Queen always carries an S-shaped metal meat hook in her bag. She places it on the table's edge and suspends her bag from it so that it doesn't touch the floor.

EVENING WEAR
Bejewelled glamour

FABULOUS JEWELLERY is an integral part of the Queen's image and she owns an incomparable private collection of personal jewels that is kept at Buckingham Palace. Her personal jewellery collection is quite distinct from the Crown Jewels, kept at the Jewel House in the Tower of London. Much of her personal collection is inherited or has been presented to her during the course of her reign. She owns some of the world's finest diamonds, as well as rubies, sapphires and emeralds.

Tiaras are an essential accessory when the Queen is in full evening dress. Some, like the Vladimir Tiara and the Cambridge Lover's Knot Tiara, were inherited from Queen Mary, who was an assiduous collector of jewellery. The Burmese Ruby Tiara was commissioned from Crown jewellers Garrard by the Queen using diamonds and rubies from her own collection. The rubies were a wedding present from the Burmese people, after whom the tiara was named.

The Girls of Great Britain and Ireland Tiara was also a wedding present for Princess May of Teck, and is familiar today from images of the Queen wearing it on banknotes and coins. It was purchased in 1893 from Garrard by a committee organised by Lady Eve Greville, and Queen Mary then gave it to her granddaughter as a wedding present in 1947. The delicate Cartier Halo Tiara was purchased by her father in 1936 as a gift for her mother. Elizabeth was given it as an 18th birthday present, and she subsequently lent the tiara to Catherine Middleton on her wedding day, 29 April 2011.

The Queen herself received many gifts of jewellery on her wedding. Her parents gave her a Boucheron diamond and ruby necklace and the Cartier King George VI chandelier earrings as wedding presents – these elaborate earrings display cut diamonds in a succession of three large drops. She had to have her ears pierced before she could wear them.

Another wedding present from her father was the George VI Victorian Suite, originally made in 1850, consisting of a long necklace of oblong sapphires surrounded by diamonds and a pair of matching square sapphire earrings. In 1952 Elizabeth had the necklace shortened, and the largest sapphire in the necklace was removed and made into a new pendant. When Sir Noël Coward saw the Queen wearing the suite at the Royal Command Performance in 1954 he wrote: "After the show we were lined up and presented to the Queen…The Queen looked luminously lovely and was wearing the largest sapphires I have ever seen".

Top left: Queen Elizabeth II, wearing a dress by Angela Kelly, at Brdo Castle for a state banquet during her state visit to Slovenia on 21 Oct 2008. She is wearing diamond bracelets on each wrist; they sit on top of her long white evening gloves, which she does not remove.

Above: The Queen, on a state visit to Qatar, wears a six-stranded pearl and diamond necklace, a gift from the Amir of Qatar. She is also wearing the Vladimir Tiara. This tiara was purchased by Queen Mary in 1921 from the collection of the Grand Duchess Vladimir, aunt of Czar Nicholas II, for whom it was made in the

1880s. It was smuggled out of Russia by British diplomats during the 1917 revolution. It comprises 15 intertwined diamond-set ovals from which hang pendant pearls. The pendant pearls can be interchanged with emeralds and the Queen has worn the tiara with both arrangements during her reign.

Above: The Queen, at a state banquet in Washington in 2007, wears the Lover's Knot brooch, a bow design with brilliant-cut diamonds set in gold and silver, bequeathed to her by Queen Mary in 1953. She is wearing the Girls of Great Britain and Ireland Tiara, and the three strand diamond festoon necklace, a wedding gift from her father.

DAY WEAR
Coordinated jewellery

JEWELLERY IS AN ESSENTIAL ACCESSORY on all occasions and, when the Queen is not required to dazzle onlookers with her diamond necklaces and tiaras at state dinners, she always has recourse to a pair of diamond and pearl stud earrings, a string of pearls and a carefully chosen brooch from her extensive collection. Sparkling diamond brooches, set against the bright colour blocks the Queen favours, always catch the eye and make her stand out.

Her grandfather King George V gave her a triple strand of pearls, when she was just nine, to celebrate his Silver Jubilee. To this day she still wears these pearls in the daytime. On the occasion of her wedding two pearl necklaces were given to Elizabeth by her father. They are known as the Queen Anne and Queen Caroline pearls, after their original owners. The combined value of the two single-row necklaces is said to be over £400,000. Famously, Elizabeth wanted to wear the necklaces on her wedding day, but belatedly discovered that they were on display – with other wedding presents – at St. James's Palace. Her private secretary Jock Colville was despatched on foot through the wedding morning throngs to retrieve the two necklaces, and their pure simplicity complemented her lavishly embroidered dress. She continues to wear the pearls for more informal evening occasions.

Brooches are the perfect complement to the Queen's hats, and always striking. In May 1858 the royal jewellers were commissioned by Queen Victoria to create three 'bow' brooches made out of 506 diamonds. These were worn by Queen Alexandra and Queen Mary at their coronations, and by the Queen Mother and Queen Elizabeth. A large pearl or diamond drop is frequently added to the brooches. Another legacy from Queen Victoria is the Golden Jubilee brooch, a festoon design of diamonds with a pearl centre and a pearl drop hanging from a looped chain of diamond collets. It was a gift to Queen Victoria in 1897 from the members of her household in celebration of her Golden Jubilee. She left it to the Crown in 1901 and it came to Queen Elizabeth in 1936.

The Queen hit the headlines on the marriage of her grandson Prince William when she was photographed wearing a bow-shaped diamond brooch with pendant tassels, known as Queen Mary's True Lover's Knot Brooch – a symbolic choice. As with all her clothes, her jewellery is seen as highly significant. When she visited Australia in 1954 she was presented with a magnificent brooch of yellow and blue-white diamonds representing the wattle, the national flower of Australia. She wore the brooch on many occasions on her first Antipodean visit and again on her recent 2011 tour.

Far left: The Queen attends the Canada Day ceremony in Ottawa on 1 July 2010. She is wearing a diamond brooch in the shape of a maple leaf, which she wore during her first visit to Canada in 1951. She subsequently lent it to the Duchess of Cambridge for her first visit to Canada in 2011.

Left: The Queen in Tuvalu, South Pacific, in 1982, wearing the Cullinan V Heart Brooch, an unusual heart-shaped stone in a diamond and platinum setting. It was bequeathed to the Queen by Queen Mary in 1953.

The Cullinan diamond, unearthed in 1905, was the largest diamond ever discovered. It weighed 3106 carats and was presented to King Edward VII by the Transvaal Government in 1907. It was insured for $1,250,000 when it was sent to England. It was subsequently cut and the nine major gemstones remain in the possession of the royal family. Queen Mary had Cullinan III and IV, known as "Granny's chips" made into a single brooch with Cullinan IV hanging from Cullinan III. It is the most valuable brooch in the world.

ANIMAL LOVER

Had she not been destined for the throne, the Queen would have liked nothing better than "to be a lady living on the country with lots of horses and dogs", as the young Lilibet once confessed to her teacher. Indeed, some of the people closest to Her Majesty agree that she gets on best with dogs, then horses, then people. Dogs have been some of her most stalwart companions since earliest childhood — both her corgis and her kennel of about 20 gundogs (labradors and cocker spaniels), while riding, keeping and breeding horses, and attending equestrian events, has been another abiding passion.

CORGIS AND DORGIS
Canine companions

The Queen is said to bring a MAGNET when she's having a dress fitted, so her BELOVED CORGIS don't get stray PINS AND NEEDLES stuck in their paws.

FROM THEIR EARLY CHILDHOOD both Elizabeth and her sister Margaret were smitten by dogs – the Queen's first ever dog, a cairn terrier, was given to her by her favourite uncle, Edward, Prince of Wales, when she was just three. But Her Majesty's famous love affair with corgis began a few years later, in 1933, when her father acquired two corgis, Dookie ('Duke of York') and Jane, in addition to his six other dogs. Besotted with their new pets, the young princesses hand-fed the corgis from a silver platter borne by a footman.

At the age of 18, the Queen received her own corgi, Susan, as a birthday gift from her father. By all accounts she was a feisty dog who over the course of time nipped various royal staff, including the royal clockwinder, a sentry and a detective. But Susan so touched her young mistress's heart that Elizabeth even took her along on her honeymoon, with the royal couple hiding her beneath travelling rugs as they drove through London in an open carriage on their way to Broadlands in Hampshire. When Susan died, at Sandringham in 1959, the Queen sketched the gravestone herself and went to great pains to find out the dog's exact birth date for the inscription, which described Susan as "for almost 15 years the faithful companion of the Queen".

The 30 corgis that the Queen has owned in her lifetime have all been direct descendants of Susan and are registered with the Kennel Club with the Windsor affix. Dorgis – corgi-dachshund crosses – made their appearance when one of the Queen's corgis, Tiny, cross-bred with Princess Margaret's dachshund Pipkin. The Queen allowed each corgi bitch one litter, and puppies that she didn't keep were given away to good homes, never sold. Her Majesty's preference has always been for corgis with a reddish tint and white underneath.

In 2009, after the death of two beloved corgis, the Queen decided to stop breeding them, since her younger dogs won't reach old age until she herself is around 90. She currently has five corgis – Monty (who was the Queen Mother's dog), Willow, Holly, Emma and Linnet – and four dorgis – Cider, Berry, Candy and Vulcan.

These priviliged pets are fed titbits from the royal table and are also each allocated a silver bowl and fed, in order of their seniority, with cooked meats, biscuits and gravy. The Queen still likes to exercise them herself when possible – indeed, it's said that if Her Majesty is wearing a headscarf when she comes into a room, the corgis dash about in excitement at their imminent walk.

HORSE BREEDER AND OWNER
Equine expertise

NOT FOR NOTHING is horse-racing called the 'sport of kings', with horses bred at the royal studs over the last two centuries winning virtually every major race in Britain. The Queen is one of the sport's greatest ambassadors of all time, as well as one of Britain's most highly regarded owners and breeders of racing thoroughbreds. Her horses have won all five Classics save the Derby, where she gained a second place with Aureole in her coronation year of 1953. Her knowledge and acumen in the field is such that her bloodstock and racing adviser John Warren once said: "The Queen is never surprised by what she is told by the trainer because she has developed the animal just like a child."

The Queen's passion for horse-racing, which took seed in childhood, was fuelled by her mother, herself a keen supporter of National Hunt racing who made many contributions to the sport, and who over half a century as an owner had more than 400 winners. In a stately gesture, the Queen covered her mother's racing expenses until her death.

As an owner, the Queen is most closely associated with Royal Ascot, where she enjoyed four winners in 1957 alone, and where, in total, she has had more than 20 winners.

Elizabeth is said to have a superb knowledge of the track, and each year travels by carriage along the main straight to get a feel of what the going is like through the noises of the wheels and the carriage horses.

She also visits training and breeding operations around the globe, squeezing them into already hectic state visits. Among them have been stallion stations and stud farms in the USA, and the National Stud in Kildare, Ireland, which she visited in 2011. The latter has always had close links with the royal family: horses raised there have won all five Classics, among them Sun Chariot, winner of the Oaks for George VI. In Ireland the Queen also visited Gilltown, the public stud of the Aga Khan, who gave her a winning filly called Astrakhan in the late 1940s. Simon Coveney, Irish agriculture minister, said: "I think the Queen is on comfortable ground here, surrounded by horsey people, many of whom she will know."

The naming of another chestnut filly Fascination speaks volumes about the way Her Majesty thinks of the horses she owns. Each season she has about 25 horses in training. They race in the royal silks: royal purple with scarlet sleeves and a black velvet cap, the inherited colours of George IV and Edward VII, fringed with gold trim and braid.

Top left: The Queen leads Carrozza and its jockey Lester Piggott into the winner's enclosure at Epsom. The filly, her first Classics winner, was triumphant in the Oaks. Two decades later, in her Silver Jubilee year of 1977, Willie Carson rode Dunfermline to victory in the Oaks. That year, the same horse and jockey ensured her victory in one of the greatest of all St. Legers.

Above: The Queen in the stableyard at Balmoral Castle in 1971, during the royal family's annual summer holiday in September 1971. The Queen is believed to have taught all of her grandchildren to ride while staying at the 20,000-hectare Scottish estate. Horses are the Queen's abiding passion. She is never happier than when she is tending to her beloved horses, watching one of her racehorses being put through its paces, riding herself, or attending annual events such as Epsom, Royal Ascot or the Badminton Horse Trials.

HORSE RIDER

An accomplished horsewoman

Left: The Queen and Ronald Reagan at Windsor Castle during the US President's state visit of 1982. The Queen is riding Burmese, while her guest rides Centennial – both horses were gifts to the Queen from the Canadian Mounted Police. Prince Philip drove Nancy Reagan behind them, in a gleaming carriage drawn by four bay horses.

Right: The Queen cantering up to the start of a 5-furlong outing with other members of the Royal Family at Ascot. The course, located just six miles from Windsor Castle, has been a favourite with the royal family since 1711.

A KEEN RIDER from early childhood, the Queen was encouraged in her love of horses by her grandfather George V, who sometimes played horse to the young girl's groom – much to the consternation of the Archbishop of Canterbury during one of his visits. The King also gave Lilibet her first pony, a Shetland called Peggy, when she was just four.

Elizabeth and her sister were taught by Horace Smith, owner of one of the major riding schools of the inter-war period, the Cadogan Riding School in Knightsbridge. Until a knee complaint forced her to give up the pastime in 2011, the Queen was particularly fond of riding early in the morning, with other members of her family, at Sandringham, Balmoral and Windsor Great Park, far from the eyes of the paparazzi.

Her best-loved mount was Burmese, a black mare that she rode for Trooping the Colour for 18 years, including during her 1981 birthday parade, when six blank shots were fired by a youth. Demonstrating that she was a highly accomplished horsewoman, the Queen was able to bring the startled mare under control despite riding sidesaddle, before comforting the steed. In 2005, she unveiled a bronze statue depicting herself mounted on Burmese in Regina, Canada.

The Queen eschews riding hats and regularly takes her place in the saddle wearing a signature headscarf.

In 2011 the Queen was photographed taking her two grandchildren, Lady Louise Windsor and Viscount Severn, for a ride; she was aged 85 at the time. The Queen's love of horses and outdoor pursuits undoubtedly contributes to her remarkable fitness and stamina.

AT THE RACES
A lifelong passion

"If it were not for my Archbishop of Canterbury, I should be off in my plane to Longchamp [a racetrack in France] every Sunday."
The Queen

RUMOURED TO READ *The Racing Post* every morning over breakfast, the Queen has been passionate about horse-racing since she was a girl. One story has it that when George VI's guide and racing manager Captain Charles Moore struggled to inform the King about the pedigree of one of his mares, Bread Card, while giving him a tour of the royal stud at Sandringham in 1938, the 12-year-old Elizabeth proudly piped up: "I know it! She is by the Derby winner Manna, out of Book Debt by Buchan!"

The Queen's knowledge of the sport is phenomenal and encyclopaedic. Indeed, according to one writer, horse-racing occupies Her Majesty's mind to such a degree that she once substituted 'National Hunt' for 'National Health Service' during her Speech to Parliament. Unsurprisingly, the Queen is rarely happier than when at the races, especially Cheltenham, the Derby and Royal Ascot. When she is too busy to attend events, the Queen catches up on big races that she has missed on video.

During the two weeks that she spends at Windsor Castle each June, she attends Ascot with family and close friends. She has not missed a year since 1945, when she was 19. The royal family attends Ascot *en masse*, arriving on course each day in a central procession of carriages before mingling with race-goers, with the Queen herself making her way down to the parade ring to get a close look at the runners. The races themselves are viewed from the Royal Box, which overlooks the Royal Enclosure lawns in line with the finishing post, and boasts a unique retractable glazed screen to allow complete visibility and capture the event's atmosphere.

The Queen's love of horse-racing is shared by many members of her family. Her mother (for whom the Queen Mother Champion Chase at the Cheltenham Festival was named) was a passionate race-goer. Her granddaughter, Zara Phillips, was voted Sports Personality of the Year in 2006 for her dressage, cross-country and show-jumping.

Watching the races allows Her Majesty to relax and to show the emotions that she often has to conceal as official head of state. As her racing manager John Warren explains: "When it comes to racing, people can really glimpse her personal side through her love for the sport." And like millions of her subjects, Her Majesty loves a flutter: in 1992, her delight at wining the royal party's Derby sweepstake – netting her the princely sum of £16 – was plain to millions of television viewers.

Top left: The Queen arrives in a horse-drawn carriage to open officially the new grandstand on the first day of Royal Ascot in 2006. Ascot has enjoyed royal patronage since the early 18th century. The first race meeting ever held at Ascot took place on 11 August 1711 and was instigated by Queen Anne. The Royal Enclosure dates back to the 1790s.

Above: The Queen and Queen Mother, both ardent horse-racing fans, watch the Derby at Epsom in 1994.

Right: The Queen, with Peter Phillips and his wife Autumn (left) and sister Zara at Royal Ascot, 2007. Within the Royal Enclosure gentlemen wear morning dress and ladies wear formal day wear.

EQUESTRIAN EVENTS
A family affair

"The welfare of Her Majesty's horses always comes first… I could ring Her Majesty at any time – day or night – to update her on the welfare of her horses."
John Warren, the Queen's bloodstock adviser

A S A MEMBER OF A HORSE-LOVING CLAN, the Queen has always been a keen spectator at equestrian events. Most important for both the Queen and the royal family as a whole is the Royal Windsor Horse Show. It was founded in 1944 by the Royal Windsor Horse Show Club, formed the previous year to host horse shows for charity, with George VI as patron. At the first show, which the young princesses attended with their parents, Elizabeth won the Single Private Driving class on her pony Hans while Margaret won the Wartime Utility Driving Class on the King's fell pony Gipsy.

Royal involvement continued as the Royal Windsor Show grew both in size and popularity. In 1952 the Queen took over her father's role as patron, and in 1954 she donated The Queen's Cup for armed services team jumping. She still attends the event each year with various members of her family, and until 2010 Prince Philip was still regularly competing in carriage-driving competitions. The Queen presented her husband the Royal Horse Society's Queen's Medal for Services to Equestrianism during the 2008 show.

The Queen has also been an enthusiastic spectator at three-day eventing, especially when her daughter Princess Anne and granddaughter Zara Phillips have been among the competitors and even winners. Anne most notably competed in the 1976 Olympic games in Montreal on the Queen's horse Goodwill. The Queen also shares this interest with the Duchess of Cornwall, whose own horses take part in showjumping, showing, general riding and cross-country trialling.

Her Majesty is also patron, and Prince Philip president, of the Guards Polo Club. From early in their relationship, the Queen was a great supporter of Philip's polo career, which took seed in his youth and culminated in him becoming one of Britain's best polo players. On their silver wedding anniversary, the monarch's gift to her husband was a bronze sculpture of him playing polo on his horse Portano.

Based in Great Windsor Park, and described by *The Polo Magazine* as the world's most prestigious polo club, Guards is most famous for hosting the star-studded Cartier International (Hurlingham Polo Association's International Day) each July. In 1985 the Queen presented an award at the event to her son Charles who, as part of the British team, beat visitors Brazil 6–5. The Queen's grandsons William and Harry have inherited their grandfather and father's passion for the sport, playing mainly at charity events.

Above left: The Queen at the third day of the Royal Windsor Horse Show in 2004.

Above: The Queen taking a photograph of her daughter Princess Anne as the latter competes in horse trials at Burghley in 1971, riding her eight-year-old gelding Doublet. She went on to become Individual Three-Day Event Champion. The Queen's granddaughter Zara Phillips made history when she took part in her first Burghley Horse Trials in 2003. She became the only child of two former winners to compete at the event, riding her horse Toytown to second place.

Above right: The Queen cheers on Prince Philip in the coach trials at the 1985 Royal Windsor Horse Show. The Prince took up carriage-driving after he retired from polo in 1971. The Queen's enthusiasm for the Royal Windsor Horse Show is undiminished: 2011 saw her enter more of her own steeds – 14 horses and ponies – than ever before.

Right: Her Majesty presents an award to Prince Charles at the Cartier International at Windsor in 1985. This is one of the most talked-about and glamorous events in the polo calendar, attracting crowds of over 25,000 people.

A Modern Monarch

Elizabeth II is the most famous woman in the world. During her long reign, she has witnessed the advent of a new egalitarianism in British society, and the end of the age of deference. She has also been subjected to an unprecedented degree of media intrusion. Yet she has continued to do her job with indefatigable dedication and good humour, and enjoys continued public popularity. In the course of her reign she has opened up and revitalised a traditionalist and hidebound institution. She has brought about major upheavals in the royal finances, opened Buckingham Palace to the public, and discarded old-established courtly rituals, such as the presentation of debutantes. She has pioneered the royal walkabout, joined Facebook, and even hosted a pop concert when she was aged 76. She is, truly, a modern monarch.

A REGAL ICON
Poise and elegance

Left: The Queen wears an evening dress designed by Norman Hartnell at the official opening of Sydney Opera House, Australia, 20 October 1973. It is made of white silk crêpe embroidered in a zig-zag pattern with pearls, sequins and beads.

Right: The Queen, photographed by Cecil Beaton, at Buckingham Palace wearing the Order of the Garter, 1953.

"I have to be seen to be believed."
Queen Elizabeth

ELIZABETH'S ACCESSION to the throne, which came when she was just 26 years old, thrust a diffident and serious young woman onto the world stage. Her sheltered childhood, spent in palaces and castles, had effectively removed her from ordinary life. She was used to having her life managed by a world of courtiers, advisers and servants. She had seen, at first-hand, her beloved father unwillingly shouldering the responsibilities of kingship, and must have been under no illusions about the hard road that stretched ahead.

But, from the age of ten, she had been made ready to embrace her destiny. She had been prepared for her royal role in myriad ways, not least by the imposing figure of Queen Mary who, with her compendious knowledge of British royal bloodlines and protocol, advised that a monarch should never allow herself to get too close to her advisers. Her marriage to Prince Philip had been a glamorous affair at a time of great gloom and austerity. In her exquisite Norman Hartnell gown, Princess Elizabeth was a beautiful bride, who glowed with new-found happiness. In the early, carefree years of her marriage, she captivated heads of state and ordinary people alike. Elizabeth and Philip were an alluring couple, much photographed and written about.

From her earliest childhood the Queen has been the subject of rapacious public interest. Even before she became Queen, she had been photographed, filmed, written about, and endured the public spotlight when she participated in state occasions, such as her father's coronation. It is scarcely surprising that, in 1953, she played her part in the elaborate theatre of the coronation with great aplomb and *sang-froid*.

Her coolness and poise are amongst her most impressive attributes. She wears her regalia well, never appearing to be dwarfed by her panoply of diamonds, garter sashes and tiaras, always maintaining an elegant, and regal, facade. Like Queen Mary before her, she understands that the public attitude to the monarchy is paradoxical; we want our Queen to be just like us, we also want her to be strikingly different.

Throughout her reign, Elizabeth has been aware that she must be the personification of both the majesty and mystery of the monarchy. Everything about her appearance is carefully choreographed; her jewellery is dazzling, her clothes are frequently symbolic, she is bedecked with the regalia of the ancient orders of chivalry. Her image has become a British icon, manifest on stamps and currency. Yet she never appears to be overwhelmed by her own symbolism.

FIGUREHEAD
The symbol of the state

"I cannot lead you into battle. I do not give you laws or administer justice but I can do something else – I can give my heart and my devotion to these old islands and to all the peoples of our brotherhood of nations."

Queen Elizabeth

THE QUEEN IS A CONSTITUTIONAL MONARCH; day-to-day power is exercised by the democratically elected government, and the Queen must be seen to be politically impartial. She symbolises the permanence and stability of the nation, removed from the ebb and flow of party politics. In the privacy of her weekly meetings with prime ministers, however, she has a right and duty to express views and – her preferred option – ask probing questions. Twelve successive prime ministers have been impressed by her intelligence and acuity, her grasp of complex issues and her awareness of the public mood.

The Queen is also the head of the Commonwealth and has been a committed supporter. She has taken a dim view of ministerial interference in her figurehead role, and has insisted on fulfilling her obligations to member states, even when her personal safety is at stake. In 1979, for example, when Prime Minister Margaret Thatcher suggested that the Queen bypassed the Commonwealth Conference in Lusaka she was firmly rebuffed. The Queen does not participate in meetings of Commonwealth leaders, but she receives them personally, and in a series of one-to-one meetings offers well-informed advice. She is also tireless in her commitment to her ceremonial role in Commonwealth countries.

The Queen also acts as an ambassador for Great Britain, promoting commercial, diplomatic and strategic relations between nation states. She has made countless keynote speeches, attended state banquets and met ordinary people the world over. Her tact and diplomacy, and her impressive stamina, is legendary.

The epic Coronation Tour, a 43,618-mile marathon, marked the beginning of her reign, imprinting her image on millions of global citizens. In 2011, aged 85, she was still demonstrating, both personally and symbolically, her ability to reconcile and unite, when she made her historic, and much-praised, state visit to Ireland.

Above: In 1994 the Queen (flanked here by President Boris Yeltsin and Patriarch Alexy II), made a highly significant visit to Russia, a symbolic end to the Cold War. In the words of Yeltsin, "monarchy can be an integral part of democratic state structure and personify spiritual and historic unity of the nation."

Right: Queen Elizabeth, wearing the Imperial State Crown, poses for a coronation photograph on 2 June 1953. The separation of pomp and politics has many supporters. George Orwell once commented that it was possible that "while this division of functions exists, a Hitler or a Stalin cannot come to power."

THE HUMAN FACE
Restraint and resilience

"Prince Philip is the only man in the world who treats the Queen simply as another human being. I think she values that. And, of course, it is not unknown for the Queen to tell the Duke to shut up."
Lord Charteris

NO ONE WOULD CALL the Queen ordinary, but she is, above all, human. She has a husband, and has been happily married for over 60 years. As a daughter, sister, mother, grandmother and great-grandmother, she has upheld and asserted her family values throughout her reign. The royal family is, in the words of Walter Bagehot, the "brilliant edition of a universal fact". They are recognisable, we can identify with them, but they exercise an enduring fascination.

The Queen grew up in a family whose life was ruled by duty and protocol. Emotions were contained and a stiff upper lip was of paramount importance. The Queen has retained these characteristics, opting for a dogged dedication to duty and avoiding displays of emotion or outright confrontation. At times, this has left her out of step with the general public; during the furore after the death of Diana, the Queen refused to break centuries of tradition and fly a standard at half-mast outside Buckingham Palace. The public mis-judged her stance, felt she was cold and unmoved, and eventually she gave way. Conversely, she was universally admired for her dignified forebearance during the difficult period when three of her children were involved in divorces and scandal swirled around the royal family.

The Queen's austerity and self-control, her protectiveness of the institution of the monarchy, and her unique symbolic position are all isolating factors. Her only confidantes are Prince Philip and a small circle of trusted friends, whose loyalty and discretion is assured. Unsurprisingly she is fascinated by everyday life and ordinary people.

Despite the relative formality of her public persona, the Queen is an excellent conversationalist, an accomplished mimic and a keen, and humorous, observer of human foibles. Over the course of her long reign she has become more serene and relaxed; her smile comes readily, and her genuine enthusiasm – whether it is for a winning horse, or for her grandson's wedding – is recognisable and infectious.

Top left: Queen Elizabeth II with Prince Charles and Princess Anne in the grounds of Balmoral Castle, 1952. Unlike most mothers, the Queen was forced to spend a great deal of her time away from her young children. Holidays in Balmoral were all about family.

Right: Queen Elizabeth II laughing as she walks with Prince Philip in Hyde Park, 2006. The couple have lived their life together in the media spotlight; the Queen would be the first to acknowledge that Prince Philip's unstinting support has been invaluable.

INDEX

INDEX

Right: The Queen wears the King George IV state diadem.

190

PICTURE CREDITS

6 Associated Press/Press Association Images
7 Empics Sports Photo Agency/Press Association Images
8 Lichfield/Getty Images
11 Illustrated London News Ltd/Mary Evans Picture Library
13cl Mary Evans Picture Library
13l © Chetham's Library, Manchester, UK/Bridgeman Art Library
13cr © British Library Board. All Rights Reserved/Bridgeman Art Library
13r National Portrait Gallery, London, UK/Bridgeman Art Library
15cl After Sir Anthony van Dyck/Getty Images
15l Stock Montage/Getty Images
15cr Hulton Archive/Getty Images
15r Studio of Sir William Beechey/Getty Images
17t Bob Thomas/Popperfoto/Getty Images
17b Charlotte Zeepvat/ILN/Mary Evans Picture Library
18l Chris Jackson/Getty Images for St James's Palace/Getty Images
18c Dylan Martinez/AFP/Getty Images
18r Indigo/Getty Images
19 Hulton-Deutsch Collection/Corbis UK Ltd.
20 Heritage Images/Corbis UK Ltd.
21 The Gallery Collection/Corbis UK Ltd.
22 Tim Graham/Getty Images
23l Mary Evans Picture Library
23r Tim Graham/Getty Images
25 Hulton-Deutsch Collection/Corbis UK Ltd.
26 Hulton-Deutsch Collection/Corbis UK Ltd.
27 Central Press/Getty Images
28 Bob Thomas/Popperfoto/Getty Images
29l Getty Images
29r Lisa Sheridan/Studio Lisa/Getty Images
30 Bob Thomas/Popperfoto/Getty Images
31 Popperfoto/Getty Images
32 Bettmann/Corbis UK Ltd.
33l Popperfoto/Getty Images
33r Popperfoto/Getty Images
34 Hulton-Deutsch Collection/Corbis UK Ltd.
35t Lisa Sheridan/Studio Lisa/Getty Images
35b Lisa Sheridan/Studio Lisa/Getty Images
36 Topical Press Agency/Getty Images
37l PA Archive/Press Association Images
37r Popperfoto/Getty Images
38 Associated Press/Press Association Images
39 Central Press/Hulton Archive/Getty Images
41 Hulton Archive/Getty Images
42 Illustrated London News Ltd/Mary Evans Picture Library
43 Hulton-Deutsch Collection/Corbis UK Ltd.
44 Reg Speller/Fox Photos/Getty Images
45t Central Press/Getty Images
45b Reg Birkett/Keystone/Getty Images
46 Keystone/Getty Images
47 V&A Images/Alamy
48 Hulton Archive/Getty Images
49 Hulton Archive/Getty Images
50 Express/Getty Images

51tl Ronald Startup/Picture Post/Getty Images
51bl John Chillingworth/Getty Images
51tr Mary Evans Picture Library
52 Loomis Dean//Time Life Pictures/Getty Images
53l Keystone-France/Gamma-Keystone/Getty Images
53r Tim Graham/Getty Images
54 Ben Curtis/AFP/Getty Images
55 Fox Photos/Getty Images
56 Bettmann/Corbis UK Ltd.
57 Carl de Souza/AFP/Getty Images
58 Sion Touhig/Getty Images
59 Fox Photos/Getty Images
60 Felipe Trueba/Epa/Corbis UK Ltd.
61 Bettmann/Corbis UK Ltd.
62 PA Wire/Press Association Images
63 PA Archive/Press Association Images
65 Lichfield/Getty Images
66 Empics Sports Photo Agency/Press Association Images
67 Hulton-Deutsch Collection/Corbis UK Ltd.
68 Associated Press/Press Association Images
69 Empics Sports Photo Agency/Press Association Images
70 Douglas Miller/Keystone/Hulton Archive/Getty Images
71 Tim Graham/Getty Images
72 Keystone-France/Gamma-Keystone/Getty Images
73 Lisa Sheridan/Studio Lisa/Getty Images
74 Empics Sports Photo Agency/Press Association Images
75 PA Archive/Press Association Images
76 Empics Sports Photo Agency/Press Association Images
77tl Associated Press/Press Association Images
77bl Empics Sports Photo Agency/Press Association Images
77tr Nils Jorgensen/Rex Features
77br Chris Jackson/Getty Images
78t Trinity Mirror/Mirrorpix/Alamy
78b Tim Graham/Getty Images
79 AFP/Getty Images
81 Associated Press/Press Association Images
82 Associated Press/Press Association Images
83l Trinity Mirror/Mirrorpix/Alamy
83r Rolls Press/Popperfoto/Getty Images
84 Trinity Mirror/Mirrorpix/Alamy
85 Associated Press/Press Association Images
86 Associated Press/Press Association Images
87l Anwar Hussein/Getty Images
87r Anwar Hussein/Getty Images
88t Trinity Mirror/Mirrorpix/Alamy
88b Tim Graham/Getty Images
89 Julian Calder/Corbis UK Ltd.
90 Tim Graham/Getty Images
91l Empics Sports Photo Agency/Press Association Images
91r Tim Graham/Getty Images
92t Samir Hussein/WireImage/Getty Images
92b Anwar Hussein/WireImage/Getty Images
93 Chris Jackson/Getty Images
95 Pool Photograph/Corbis UK Ltd.
96t PA Wire/Press Association Images

96b Tim Graham/Getty Images
97 Empics Sports Photo Agency/Press Association Images
98 Stefan Rousseau/AFP/Getty Images
99t Empics Sports Photo Agency/Press Association Images
99b Central Press/Getty Images
100 Andrew Parsons/AFP/Getty Images
101 Tim Graham/Getty Images
102 Empics Sports Photo Agency/Press Association Images
103t Empics Sports Photo Agency/Press Association Images
103b Pool/Tim Graham/Getty Images
104 Pool Photograph/Corbis UK Ltd.
105 Bettmann/Corbis UK Ltd.
106 Empics Sports Photo Agency/Press Association Images
107l Keystone/Getty Images
107r PA Archive/Press Association Images
108 Keystone Pictures USA/Alamy
109 Pool Photograph/Corbis UK Ltd.
110 PA Wire/Press Association Images
111t Pool/Anwar Hussein/Getty Images
111b Tim Graham/Getty Images
113 PA Archive/Press Association Images
114 Hulton Archive/Getty Images
115t Lawrence Jackson/White House/Corbis UK Ltd.
115b Lisa Sheridan/Studio Lisa/Getty Images
116 iStockphoto/Thinkstock
117 Associated Press/Press Association Images
118t Ron Bell/PA Archive/Press Association Images
118b Peter King/Fox Photos/Getty Images
119 Terry O'Neill/Getty Images
120 Keystone-France/Gamma-Keystone/Getty Images
121t PA Archive/Press Association Images
121b Central Press/Getty Images
122 Tim Graham/Getty Images
123t Tim Graham/Getty Images
123b Tim Graham/Getty Images
124 Associated Press/Press Association Images
125l Jim Gray/Keystone/Getty Images
125r Martin Rickett/PA Archive/Press Association Images
127 John Stillwell/WPA Pool/Getty Images
128 Isobel Peachey/Arthur Edwards/AFP/Getty Images
129 Camera Press
130 Jane Bown/Camera Press
131 Cecil Beaton/V&A Images/Alamy
132 Shaun Curry/AFP/Getty Images
133 Associated Press/Press Association Images
134 Clive Dixon/Rex Features
135l Oli Scarff/Getty Images
135r © money & coins @ ian sanders/Alamy
136 Vintage Image/Alamy
137t Hulton Archive/Getty Images
137b Lamb/Alamy
139 Associated Press/Press Association Images
140 PA Archive/Press Association Images

141 Associated Press/Press Association Images
142 Fox Photos/Getty Images
143 AFP/Getty Images
144 Ian Jones Photography Ltd.
145 Ted Blackbrow/Daily Mail/Rex Features
146 Alastair Muir/Rex Features
147 AF archive/Alamy
149 Tim Graham/Getty Images
150l Keystone/Hulton Archive/Getty Images
150r Popperfoto/Getty Images
151 Central Press/Getty Images
152l Tim Graham/Getty Images
152r Tim Graham/Getty Images
153l Tim Graham/Getty Images
153r Tim Graham/Getty Images
154t Tim Graham/Getty Images
154b Tim Graham/Getty Images
155 Tim Graham/Getty Images
156t Christopher Furlong/WPA/Pool/Getty Images
156b Rupert Hartley/David Hartley/Rex Features
157 Irish Government/Pool/Getty Images
158 Tim Rooke/Rex Features
159 Andrew Winning/WPA Pool/Getty Images
160 Adam Woolfitt/Corbis UK Ltd.
161l Chris Jackson/Getty Images
161r Tim Graham/Getty Images
162 Tim Graham/Getty Images
163 Tim Graham/Getty Images
164 Tim Rooke/Rex Features
165l Reginald Davis/Rex Features
165r Anwar Hussein/FilmMagic/Getty Images
166 Tim Rooke/Rex Features
167 Tim Graham/Getty Images
169 Associated Press/Press Association Images
170 Bettmann/Corbis UK Ltd.
171 Anwar Hussein/Getty Images
172 Central Press/Getty Images
173 Lichfield/Getty Images
174 Georges De Keerle/Getty Images
175 Bentley Archive/Popperfoto/Getty Images
176 Scott Barbour/Getty Images
177t Empics Sports Photo Agency/Press Association Images
177b Rex Features
178 Carl De Souza/Getty Images
179tl Bettmann/Corbis UK Ltd.
179tr Hulton-Deutsch Collection/Corbis UK Ltd.
179br Hulton-Deutsch Collection/Corbis UK Ltd.
181 Empics Sports Photo Agency/Press Association Images
182 Anwar Hussein/Getty Images
183 V&A Images/Alamy
184 Martin Keene/PA Archive/Press Association Images
185 Keystone-France/Gamma-Keystone/Getty Images
186 Lisa Sheridan/Studio Lisa/Getty Images
187 Tim Graham/Getty Images
191 Tim Graham/Getty Images
Cover Bettmann/Corbis UK Ltd.